GLENDURGAN

A Personal Memoir of a Garden in Cornwall

by Charles Fox

With best wishes

Charles

Here is to Truro

Trelissick
Davies Gilbert

RIVER FAL

CARRICK ROADS

Perran
Chas. Fox

Carclew
Sir Chas. Lemon

Enys
John Enys

Roscrow
Robt. Were Fox, Sen.

Flushing

Leadeth to Helston

FALMOUTH

Friends' Burial Grd.

Pendennis Castle

Budock Water

Penmere
W. Fenwick

Penjerrick
Robt. Were Fox

FALMOUTH BAY

Tregedna
Joshua Fox

G. C. Fox & Co.

Grove Hill
(Geo. Croker Fox)

Glendurgan
Alfred Fox

Trebah
Chas. Fox

Rosehill
(Robt. Were Fox)

Wodehouse Place
Alfred Fox

HERE IS HELFORD RIVER

Bank House
Mrs. R. W. Fox Sen.

NARE POINT

CONTENTS

Left: Map showing main Fox gardens, and other connected properties
Title page: A Victorian letter

To Alfred Fox Esq
Kind Sir, will you admit or not,
My humble lines within your Grot
They're written with a good intent
All future mischief to prevent
From your petitioner N. W.
Who promises no more to trouble you.
Glendurgan 10 September 1846

Stranger! If this thy happy lot,
Whilst rambling here, to find this peaceful spot,
On seats prepared to give the weary rest,
Thou may'st in quietude be truly blest,
Then O! be grateful for the bliss enjoy'd,
Nor let the generous Owner be annoy'd
By finding things that ornament and grace
This rural grot – be taken out of place.
Remove no specimen! Pull off no cone!
Stir not the Foxes! Leave the moss alone!
And when time bids thee from the Glen depart,
If thou hast not a cold and senseless heart
Warm aspirations will to Heav'n ascend
For blessings on that kind indulgent friend
Who aided nature, with his own good taste,
And made an Eden spring, in Durgan's waste;
Nor acting from a narrow, selfish mind
Has he, its beauties, to the few confin'd,
But with benevolence that knows no bounds
Permits the public, to enjoy his grounds..

FOREWORD
by TIM SMIT

When I was asked to write a foreword to this marvellous book I felt a bit like a fraud, not being a great gardener. However, the chance to sing the praises of one of my favourite gardens and the family which has shaped Cornish horticulture more than any other was too good to pass up.

I went to school next to Vita Sackville-West's garden at Sissinghurst in Kent and I have warm, if slightly guilty memories of breaking in and stealing my first kiss by moonlight in the White Garden there. Perhaps subliminally gardens for me have never been about the pleasure of horticulture; they have always been about capturing spirit of place and romance. There are many famous garden owners, landscape architects and garden makers who over the years have turned Britain into probably the world's capital of the art of gardening. However, there can be few, if any, families which have had such a profound effect as the Fox family.

When the restoration of what became known as the Lost Gardens of Heligan began, I spent countless hours trawling through the archives of both the Tremayne family, its owners, and the Cornwall Garden Society. I was transported by the Show reports which were dominated by the competition to grow the finest blooms and crops, both domestic and exotic. One name seemed to dominate – Fox. Curious, I made a pilgrimage to Falmouth to explore the impact of this family. The great influence of the scientist Robert Were Fox FRS, who was fascinated by the possibilities for growing tender exotic species in this mild climate, shaped Cornish gardens more than anything else. In Falmouth, Rosehill which he leased in the 1820s was the testing ground, and it was here that many of the competition winners were grown; but this was not a great garden in the aesthetic sense. If Rosehill was the laboratory, the fruits of these experiments championed by his son, nephew and grandsons can be seen at Penjerrick, Trebah and Glendurgan, as fine a group of valley gardens as have ever been created. Of these, Glendurgan was the jewel in the crown.

Remarkably, only three Head Gardeners served Glendurgan from the 1830s to the 1960s. Surely nowhere else can match such longevity, which perhaps explains the serenity of Glendurgan. Unusually for Cornish gardens the design isn't cramped by over-planting, the specimens have air around them, and can be enjoyed without the feeling of breathless excitement so often found elsewhere. It is a garden sure of itself, with an integrity of design, where ambitious planting never dominates the composition.

Great plants, great design, great tradition and … a great future. Glendurgan is a national treasure for which we have to thank the Foxes.

Durgan, with Glendurgan above

PREFACE

*'The land produced vegetation: plants bearing seed according
to their kinds and trees bearing fruit with seed in it according
to their kinds. And God saw that it was good.'*

(Genesis 1: 12)

I write this book partly as the result of various pleas, but more because of a passion that I have for the place and its flora, and an enthusiasm for sharing that passion with others. My only qualifications are that I happen to be one of the many great-great grandchildren of Alfred Fox, who was responsible for the birth of Glendurgan. I have drawn considerably from his journal, and also that of his son, George; I have had further access to a large amount of unpublished material; and, perhaps most relevantly, I have known personally many of the characters involved. I was brought up and now live at Glendurgan, and in this way have a degree of first-hand knowledge, which according to my parents started at the age of three when I was able to identify some flowers on the table as being *Choisya ternata*. With this early love of plants, a fascination for the designs of nature, an ability to draw, and later an aptitude for Latin, it was with some advantage that I went on to become a garden designer. However, I readily confess to the fact that the more I know the more I realize how little I know.

What I have endeavoured to produce is neither a straight dendrological account, nor a colourless guidebook, but more a personal insight into the history and character of the garden. I make no bones about being prejudiced in favour of the National Trust, whose careful ownership has contributed much towards my involvement and inspiration.

The book is written thematically. It starts by looking at the background of the Cornish garden, Cornwall's climate and geography, progressing to the effects of the industrial revolution in the nineteenth century. It then moves into the Quaker nature of the Fox family and its motivation, followed by a chapter on children, who are the garden's greatest users. Many of my own reminiscences centre around this aspect of the garden. The chronology is then picked up under the headings of 'Duty' and 'Change', divided by two chapters devoted solely to gardening matters. No subject, however, is exclusive to its own chapter, and throughout I have deliberately kept references going to both people and plants.

The illustrations are selected to support the text, and not merely to be ornamental. There are a couple of maps – one showing the proximity of Fox properties in the Falmouth area, and the other showing the layout of the garden. There is also a family tree, pruned for the purposes of this book, and a key to the family for those who become completely perplexed.

I would like to make a number of acknowledgements. The book could not have been published without the support and encouragement of the National Trust, and under that banner I would like to thank the following for reading the manuscript: John Sales, ex Gardens Adviser; Emma Tennant, ex Chairman of the Gardens Panel; Jeremy Pearson, Historic Buildings Consultant; Chris Curtis, property manager for Glendurgan; Steven Porter, Head Gardener at Glendurgan, and his two assistant gardeners. For botanical accuracy I am indebted to Tony Lord. Many of the photographs I took myself, but for some I need to thank the National Trust, and Liz Luck at the Cornwall Regional Office, in particular for those on pages 28 and 107. I must thank profusely Tony Kent who was ready to meet at dawn or dusk and take photographs at my exacting direction. Other photographs, of archival material, were taken by Lucinda Withinshaw and Sharon Jefford, who were equally professional. I am grateful to Rupert Tenison for allowing me to reproduce his photograph of Trewithen; to Melanie Eclare for that of Chyverton and to Douglas Pett for those on pages 42 and 97. Some of the prints are reproduced with permission of John Maggs, the print dealers in Falmouth. The family tree on page 118 is reproduced by permission of Douglas Pett, and the plan on pages 116–17 by permission of Eric Thomas/The National Trust. At the last moment John Such of Scanair UK zoomed in with the aerial photograph reproduced on page 6. My brother William also supplied some photographs, and was an expert proof-reader. Further members of the family to be subjected to this invaluable task were my father, Philip, and my wife, Caroline. I am grateful to my distant cousin Sarah Smith for several illustrations, to D.M. Thomas for a poem by him about the garden, to Charles Thomas for finding a poem about Joshua Fox, and to Sue Pring for telling me about the Men of Trees. A huge debt is owed to two individuals, who mercifully took a schoolmaster's approach to the manuscript: Douglas Pett, author of *The Parks and Gardens of Cornwall*, and other garden-related publications, and Pamela Richardson, whose knowledge of and enthusiasm for the history of the family is unbounded as well as scholarly. I need to express my appreciation to the owners of the other two main Fox gardens – Trebah Gardens Trust, synonymous with Tony Hibbert, and my cousin Rachel Morin, of Penjerrick.

On the professional front I would like to thank my literary agent, William Neill-Hall, and Tim Smit who generously agreed to write the Foreword. For her faith in the project, for her sensitivity and professionalism, I am grateful to my publisher Alison Hodge, and for his imaginative interpretation of the material I thank Christopher Laughton, who designed the book. Finally for proof-reading, and for encouragement I would like to thank Philip Marsden, whose own books have been an inspiration, and who lit the first flame for *Glendurgan: A Personal Memoir of a Garden in Cornwall*.

Note that all the photographs are of Glendurgan unless otherwise stated.

'At Rosehill the banana, the citron and the orange have been grown in the open for several years; dracaenas 20–25 feet high are of common occurence; and from one end of the grounds to the other surprises in the way of exotic plants fall so thick and fast that the visitor really begins to doubt his senses. Without any protection, abutilons have reached a height of 20 feet, nicotiana colossea [tomentosa] 14 feet, and datura sanguinea a diametre of 14 feet and a height of 9 feet.'

(*Hamilton Davey, in the* Journal of the Royal Institution, *1897*)

Glendurgan, 1826

Glendurgan is a sheltered valley garden running down to Durgan on the shores of the River Helford in south-west Cornwall. In the beginning the land was moorland on which only a few trees grew. The two plants that grew in proliferation, and which would have been appreciated by the people of Durgan, were gorse, which was used for fuel, and willows, which were used for making crab pots and baskets. Even in the early twentieth century the character of a Durgan allotment would be marked by a bed of withies. Around the hamlet were a handful of orchards, which must also have contributed to the villagers' subsistance.

The garden was started in the early 1820s by Alfred Fox (1794–1874), and by 1826 he had built a small, thatched cottage at the top of the valley. In 1837 this was the victim of a serious fire, as is recorded by Barclay Fox, his brother Robert's son:

> Was engaged to Grove Hill to dinner, but at 4 o'clock was met by the intelligence that *Glendurgan* was on fire. Rode there directly with Uncle Alfred. We found the tragedy there concluded & the four smoking walls with a smokeless chymney (sic) at either end all that remained of its former magnificence. The crowd of villagers there assembled were eager in their condolences with his Honour (Uncle A.) who showed himself the hero throughout & caused, I imagine, admiration & wonder. He was the merriest of the party, looked on the bright side of it & gave all the operatives some porter, which was the finest trait of all. We found nearly all the furniture saved & stowed away in the loft over the stable. Nobody knows how it happened. The thatch caught first & it is conjectured that it was occasioned by a spark. It was not insured.

The house was subsequently rebuilt on a slightly larger scale, with a caretaker's cottage at the back, and then in 1891, the year after Alfred's widow had died, extended by his son George Fox (1845–1931). Planting was continued by his descendants Cuthbert Fox (1885–1972), and Philip Fox (born 1922), followed by the National Trust, to whom Glendurgan was given in 1962.

The garden is one of three valley gardens created by three brothers, the other two being Penjerrick and Trebah, which were respectively the inspiration of Robert the elder, and Charles the younger. Alfred was a man of business; Charles a man of letters, and Robert a man of science: he invented the dipping needle that pinpoints the centre of the Earth. All three brothers were partners in the family business. At that time this included timber, fishing, and mining interests, as well as the Falmouth ship agency, which continues today.

Alfred Fox

Robert Fox

J. F. TRULL   Charles Fox   FALMOUTH

All three gardens have views of the sea; whether this was with an eye to any potential business that might come sailing over the horizon is not known. In 1882 a national journal recorded that from Penjerrick 'stretching away into the hazy distance is the blue English Channel, on whose waters the homeward and outward-bound vessels are continually in sight'.

The sea is now romantically obscured by the branches of mature trees. To note a charming difference from the other two gardens, Penjerrick is divided by a 'hollow lane, whose banks are densely covered with indigenous ferns and crossed by a rustic bridge', the lane twisting below sometimes being referred to by the family as the London road – either a sarcastic allusion to its diminutive size, or perhaps because of the illusion of gaudy high-street colour that borders it in spring. Originally the view from Glendurgan was open towards the mouth of the River Helford.

Penjerrick, 1870

Penjerrick today

Glendurgan in the late 19th century

Now it is restricted to a triangle. Intriguingly, this was also once the case with Trebah, whereas today from the bottom of that garden there is the bonus of a second view looking back at the house.

The Fox family originated in Wiltshire, and according to the family crest, but tenuously, from the same stem as the Earls of Ilchester. In the early seventeenth century a branch splintered to the west, establishing itself as Quaker merchants in Fowey, and residing for a time near Liskeard at a place called Catchfrench. There is no evidence to suggest that the family was related to the George Fox who was born in 1624, and who became the founder of that group of people mockingly named Quakers; they called themselves the 'Society of Friends'. It was coincidental that the Cornish Foxes were Quakers, and seemed to have a liking for the name of George.

In the mid-eighteenth century George Croker Fox moved his business from Fowey to Falmouth at a very advantageous time in the town's history. For a start, religious sects such as Quakers and Jews were tolerated in this area, given a place in society, and able to make an economic contribution to the community. In those days Falmouth was more like a village, and the properties the family owned were substantial houses with large gardens situated on the outskirts of the town. They began at Bank House on the water's edge in 1759, and then spread up the hill. Grove Hill House, the property of George Croker Fox, had an oval walled

garden and a small deer park. It had a long drive and a lodge in the form of a Swiss cottage, the occupant of which had the onerous job of shutting and opening the front gate by the invisible means of a long piece of string. It is a sad indictment of the twentieth century that properties such as these, which once led delightfully from the centre of towns into the landscape beyond, became lost in seas of urban development.

Rosehill, which became the property of Robert Were Fox, had a garden that could accommodate more than 300 exotic species of lemon. These have not stood the test of time, but the garden donated by the family to Falmouth Art

School, and now part of Falmouth College of Art, is nonetheless worth a visit.

The generations that followed George Croker spread over the region, and started or became involved in many varied businesses. They used their connections within the family to great benefit and being Quakers, married exclusively and judiciously within their own religious sect. They were, for example, closely and conveniently related to the banking families of both Lloyd and Barclay. Being enthusiastic and diligent gardeners in theory and in practice, they also used opportunities in the shipping and travel world to introduce rare and exotic plants to the gardens for which they were responsible in and around Falmouth: Rosehill, Grove Hill, Tredrea, and Goonvrea, as well as Penjerrick and Trebah, which are as celebrated as Glendurgan, the subject of this book.

The Foxes may have been good businessmen and endowed with more than reasonable intellect, but they were modest in their attitudes, which were governed by a healthy respect for the sacredness of life. Self-gratification was not part of their psychological make-up – a relevant fact when admiring their gardens as they are today in all their fame and glory. In Falmouth and elsewhere they built and owned houses simply as a matter of course: houses that were practical for use by both family and business. Some modern historians purport that the Foxes possessed fine properties because they were men of wealth, seeking to make an impact on the landscape. There were in Cornwall others who did this, and there are others who continue to do so, but with the Foxes this was not their way. The paradox is that today some of their town houses do contrast dramatically with encroaching tiers of bungalows.

The two defiant little houses on the foreshore at Durgan, exceptionally, were the inspiration and product of one of Alfred and Sarah Fox's sons-in-law, Sir Joseph Pease. It was the age of British supremacy, and of prosperity for some, such as the Peases, who were successful Quaker businessmen from Darlington. It was not surprising that Joseph in his steam yacht *Rosebery*, on a visit to the ancient fishing village of Durgan, should in true Victorian style wish to impose a stamp of prestige and authority over the elements. Above their battered sea walls the two edifices have windows that look bravely out to sea. The customary way of building cottages by the sea was to recess them, with the side exposed to the roughest weather featuring neither door nor window.

It is a matter of accident rather than intention that some of the Foxes' properties have now become the subject of public gaze, a fact which is vital to grasp for any deep understanding of the origins of their gardens. To put it another way, it is doubtful that even a hundred years ago any member of the family would have been tempted into contemplating what the family had achieved, in terms of either business or gardens. Unlike today, it was not the fashion and certainly not their fashion. It seems that people lived much more for the present than the past; and the Foxes were particularly good at this, and at not worrying about the morrow.

Three criteria govern the style of gardening in this part of the British Isles. First, Cornwall is minerally one of the richest counties in the country, with an abundance of slate and granite, turning the soil acidic. Second is climate. Technically, it is not the Gulf Stream but the North Atlantic Drift, together with 45 inches of rain per year, that makes it possible to grow so many semi-exotic and semi-hardy plants. In other words, as John Norden so charmingly wrote in his *Topographical and Historical Description of Cornwall* of 1584:

> To recompense this banished promontorie with the supply of
> another mean, Nature hath so confined it, as that the seas saltiness,
> sendeth warme enapurations which cherisheth the earth as with a
> contynuall sweete deaw, which yealdeth unto the earthes increase
> quick maturitye, and preventeth the bitterness of the nipping froste,
> which cannot long contynue violent, nor the moste contynuying fall
> of the thickninge snowe make a daungerous deepness to remayne
> longe, in regard of the seas heate meltinge it in the fall: But the
> fierce and furious wyndes sharply assayle the naked hills and Dales,
> havinge no defensive woodes for shelter… The greatest wante that
> the Countrye hath is woode and timber… .

In the years since the Foxes acquired Glendurgan many shelter belts have been created to provide those 'defensive woods'.

One result of this benign climate is that, as Frederick Hamilton Davey put it, writing in the early days of Penjerrick, in *The Cornish Magazine*:

> you can be sure of finding many a cheerful bloom the whole winter
> through… acacias and deutzias unfurl their streamers weeks before
> they are seen in the midlands; and many a rhododendron and azalea
> is kissed into flower when northern gardens are still swathed in
> snow.

It is not only the proliferation of exotic plants that is impressive; it is the way in which they combine with each other, and with our native species. In 1899 Penjerrick was described as a 'chaos of Himalayan rhododendrons mixed with plants from New Zealand and branches from the Rockies' – words which

Penjerrick

illustrate how important, incidentally, that particular garden was and is as a repository for plants from all over the globe.

Many plants in this favourable climate will grow to record-breaking size. Hamilton Davey wrote of Penjerrick that 'plants which are the glory of the equatorial belt here attain the status of giants', and of the massive European beech which sadly no longer adorns the same garden, Alan Mitchell the tree expert is quoted as saying to the owner '*Fagus sylvatica* 'Pendula' – easily the tallest, biggest and finest of its kind in Britain. No other specimen is comparable'. In 1831 Alfred recorded that he had 'gathered a gooseberry 4¼ inches in circumference'. George too was fond of records. In 1897 he wrote 'Billy brought in citrus, one measured 1' 10½" round the long way and 1' 9' the short way (the waist). It would just squeeze into my hat endways but would not go in the long way'. For the last 20 years of the twentieth century *Populus* 'Androscoggin' at Glendurgan has been the fastest growing recorded tree in any National Trust property.

The third criterion governing the style of gardening in Cornwall is the indigenous landscape. As the *Western Morning News* so eloquently put it, on 28 September 1927:

Cornish gardens, based as they are on the old English landscape style, owe a great deal to the lie of the land. The little Cornish valley, beginning almost imperceptibly on the hilltop and becoming a deep glen with startling precocity, is the nucleus of many of our finest gardens… The northern shores of that lovely inlet known as Helford Haven have a fine series of modern gardens in the sheltered vallies (sic) leading down to it. They have grown up and decked the landscape in less than a century.

Cornish gardens can be said to be arranged for great effect, in contrast to flatter parts of England where it is possible and often desirable to impose a formal design on the landscape, as at Hampton Court. In the same way as fenland lends itself to formal avenues, so hills and valleys lend themselves to informal woodland gardens. As Sarah Fox said to her son George in 1890 'there was', at Glendurgan, 'no original design for the grounds but it gradually worked into what it now is'. Some Cornish gardens, however, have perhaps a small area, or feature, which shows evidence of the designer's hand; there are two notable examples. The first is at Trebah where Charles Fox, a keen sinologist, employed the art of Geomancy, or Feng Shui, to determine planting positions: apparently 16 gardeners, a good deal of scaffolding, and a loud hailer were used to produce the effect that trees might have on reaching maturity, to ensure that they were planted in exactly the right places. Glendurgan, its neighbouring garden, does not seem to have suffered from lack of this technique. The second is Trewithen where, unusually for Cornwall, the garden is mostly level. An elegant and important garden, it was consciously redesigned by George Johnstone this side of 1900, without the contrivance of avenue or equestrian statue, and again relying for success on the ability to grow exotic trees and shrubs to immense proportions.

Populus 'Androscoggin'

Trewithen

Chyverton

Tredrea

Trelissick

Many advances in gardening owe their existence to Cornwall's industrial revolution of the eighteenth and nineteenth centuries. The mainsprings of this were the copper and tin mining industries. They had a two-fold effect. A demand for pit props had led to coppicing and the denudation of oak woods. So severe did this become that in 1800 John Thomas of Chyverton summoned a group of landowners who resolved to plant trees, and who became known as 'The Men of Trees'. Their initiative is well reflected by the superb plantsman's collection of trees, magnolias in particular, which can be seen today at Chyverton, even if it has to be said that most of them were planted this side of 1900.

For many families, such as the Foxes, the age of prosperity also embraced other activities such as railways, foundries, and the construction of ports and breakwaters. Evidence of the success of businessmen could be detected through their gardens. From their houses there was often a commanding view of the source of their income: Hitchins and Drew in their *History of Cornwall* (1824) referred to Tredrea, which overlooked the Foxes' foundry at Perranarworthal, and at one time belonged to Charles Fox of Trebah: 'The plantations raised round the abode of Mr Fox, thrive with peculiar luxuriance, and give variety to the diversified scenery, which arises from the effects of labour and machinery', meaning the employment of about 400 men.

For some the views were of tin mines, with perhaps open park-land in the foreground. Often, and in a grand throwaway gesture, the garden would be sited at a distance from the source of their wealth, for instance at Tregothnan, Trelissick, Carclew or Lanhydrock.

Cotehele

Historically, views of the sea were not common for large Cornish houses: previously many country houses, such as the last two mentioned, or the ancient mansions of Cotehele in east Cornwall and Trelowarren on the Lizard peninsula, were built inland far from fierce sea gales and the prying eyes of pirates and smugglers.

But the wooded valley garden soon became the Victorian stamp of affluence. This was the equivalent of the great bedding-out schemes to be admired in large English gardens at the time, especially in the industrial parts of the Midlands and North country, schemes which, although once common in the larger Cornish houses such as Carclew, are now seen only in municipal parks and hotels. One notable exception is the National Trust's faithfully Victorian planting at Lanhydrock.

It would seem, however, that what drove the Fox family was not vaulting ambition, but rather an innate love of and respect for all things natural. There was also a liberating, creative aspect to gardening; indeed, for the ladies, maybe their garden sketches were born of the repressive discipline of Quakerism. Unlike so many of their contemporaries, for whom the countryside represented agriculture, hunting and shooting, and the rather hazardous territory over which one walked miles in order to work – and Barclay Fox does make many references to trudging,

Lanhydrock

Pencalenick

traipsing, and ploughing – the Foxes were more like some of the writers and artists of the day: individuals who loved and appreciated the countryside for its own intrinsic values. In contrast to this a member of another Cornish family, which owned a breathtakingly beautiful estate, Pencalenick, on the edge of an estuary, once said of his childhood in the early twentieth century, 'We never left the terraces' – except, he omitted to mention, in pursuit of animals.

The Foxes were quiet, gentle people, but with strong iron fists in velvet gloves. This is a characteristic to be observed throughout the family, as is well testified in the following obituary of Howard Fox of Rosehill. He was one of Alfred's sons, and died in 1922:

Howard Fox

True it is that he was one of the best scientists of his native county, and interested in all solid work for its good; but this does not convey the true sense of his sterling quality and friendliness. To a rock-like firmness of will and stability of character was joined an absolute straightforwardness which I have never found equalled; and yet so great and fine were his natural courtesy and kindliness of spirit that one never felt asperity in the strength of mind, and his blue eyes could fill with the friendliest light when comforting, with grave quietness anyone who was worried with the strains of life.

In this particular story, such was the type of person to be entrusted with the gentle evolution of both a business and a garden.

FALMOUTH FOR ORDERS
CHAPTER TWO

'Captain Fitzroy came to tea.
He returned yesterday from five
years' voyage in HMS BEAGLE.'
(The diary of Caroline Fox, 1 October 1836)

Falmouth, c. 1850

There is no doubt that from 1700 to about 1850 Falmouth was one of the busiest, if not the busiest, port in the country. The reason for this is that Falmouth is one of the largest natural harbours in the world; it is the first and last port of call in the English Channel; and until the advent of the steam train it handled all the incoming and outgoing mail for most of northern Europe. In addition, the French wars caused overseas trade to be concentrated here, rather than risk running the gauntlet of enemy shipping further up the channel. On occasions Falmouth was so busy that it was possible to walk from one side of the harbour to the other – if you could see it – stepping from boat to boat. One day in the winter of 1847 Alfred counted 190 vessels in the bay alone. News and fashions from the continent frequently came to Falmouth first. Men made money, and the buildings in Falmouth now regarded as fine examples of late eighteenth or early nineteenth century architecture were no more than the relatively modest villas of their day. This was in accordance with what was happening in the Cornish countryside and elsewhere in England: the *nouveau riche* were fast becoming gentrified, and what are now regarded as stately homes were once the fanciful enterprises of men of humble origin, but blessed by competitive spirit and quite phenomenal income.

For an old-fashioned, family-run company, which radiated centuries of stability rather than high technology, G.C. Fox & Co. always kept abreast of the times. In the 1870s they laid the first telegraphic line from Falmouth to the Lizard for the advance warning of ships, and subsequently they have always been among the first to invest in the latest forms of communication. It was as a consequence of their ship agency business that the family met a great many illustrious visitors who needed to be entertained. The journals of the diarists, Caroline and Barclay Fox, the children of Robert Were Fox who owned Penjerrick, describe the visits of individuals such as Byron, Tennyson, Wordsworth, Carlyle and Sterling. Bank House, Robert Were Fox's town house, offered hospitality to the Queen of Portugal, and in April 1840 Alfred recorded that 'the two Ashanti princes and their tutor dined at Glendurgan'. These are not claims to fame, but aim to give some idea of what was happening in the area at that time, by good chance for the Fox family. Of Quaker stock, the Foxes were very much *vin ordinaire*, and as is so common with non-conformists, from the purple of commerce, and little versed in courtly observances. Yet they remained unfazed at having to mingle with the grandees of society – what is touching was that the Queen of Portugal had objected to being decked out for the occasion, knowing she was going to visit a family where plainness of dress was the norm. Queen Victoria, who came to Falmouth in 1846, may have been briefed in advance that she was going to meet a man whose religious beliefs would prevent him from removing his hat, in spite of being a loyal and, as recorded by the Queen herself, gift-bearing subject – it was a grapefruit. The Quaker belief was that because all men are equal in the eyes of God, honour had to be given to Him alone, and therefore special distinctions, in this instance a mere queen, ought not to be recognized. Fortunately the day turned out to be so hot he 'simply could not keep it on'.

In due course, with the expansion of their families, and maybe a sense of crowding and too much activity in Falmouth, some members of the family felt inspired to invest in properties outside the town. Undoubtedly this was connected to material success, although not necessarily to a desire to flaunt it; on the whole this meant nothing to them, even if they did become more worldly in dress, possessions and habits. Principally their country retreats were for recreational activities, but the productivity of the land, such as orchards at

Durgan, would also have entered the equation – the family enjoyed growing fruit trees. There was another magnet: at one time G.C. Fox & Co. had serious interests in the fishing industry, particularly in pilchards. A natural diversification was to invest in fish cellars all around the coast of Cornwall, and it is just possible that the hamlet of Durgan on the River Helford provided such an outlet.

Fish cellars, Durgan

There are pilchard pressing stones to be found along the Schoolroom Walk at Glendurgan. In 1923 a Durgan man, John Downing, then in his eighties, recalled how the reading room's quay walls were once the same as the old cellar, which had a big door on the south side for rolling pilchard casks over a staging on to a vessel for shipment.

A further reason for the move from Falmouth could have been to escape disease. There were certainly outbreaks of cholera in the port, and other ship-borne contagions were always likely. The expansion of the Fox gardens was partly due to the family's shipping connections, which meant that to a small extent the partners in the business may have commissioned ships' captains to bring them seeds from all over the world. For example, although it is not known whether he received specific instructions from the family, it is said that the few remaining monkey puzzle trees along the drive at Penjerrick grew from seeds imported from South America by Archibald Menzies and William Lobb, whose introduction of this

Monkey puzzles, Penjerrick

genus enriched many other Cornish gardens. When Darwin's Captain Fitz-roy, who has now, incidentally, had a sea area named after him, came to tea he brought with him a present in the form of a brain coral, which still holds its place in the garden at Penjerrick.

Another, probably apocryphal story is that the introduction of tree ferns to this country was the result of some trunks which apparently had been destroyed in a bush fire near Adelaide in South Australia, and which were then used as ballast in a ship that came to Falmouth. On arrival, they were

Brain coral, Penjerrick

observed to have sprouted, and were planted, thus changing the face of the Cornish garden landscape. In the early twentieth century George recorded that he and other members of the family received from an Italian fishing contact (the firm exported pilchards to Italy) a gift of olive trees, a genus which the National Trust has recently reintroduced to Glendurgan with considerable success.

Members of the family also acted in an honorary capacity as consuls for as many as 36 different countries, which may also have widened and strengthened their contacts abroad, as well as making them, and their properties, amenable to visitors. In the summer of 1848 Alfred wrote that 'a steamer brought 39 German Captains and the wives of three of them to Glendurgan to dine with us, in all about 64 at dinner on the lawn. A delightful day.'

Olive trees, Glendurgan

Prince Axel of Denmark and his officers being entertained by the family in the garden at Rosehill, 1912

QUAKER HEIRS
THE FIRST GENERATION
CHAPTER THREE

'In gracious splendour now, colours and sounds
Seem like the breath of God, where He abounds
In beauty and in peace, for He has made
A Benediction here and He has stayed
The Angels in their flight that they might see
One spot on earth embrace this sovereignty.'

(Friend of the family)

Glendurgan

It is increasingly being realized that the collection of plants and the gentle art of gardening can lead to feelings of peace and contemplation. As an expression of this it almost became a Quaker tenet to establish a Heaven on Earth – perhaps rather a loose interpretation of Biblical instructions to cultivate a garden.

This predominant trait, this quest for the divine, may account for the countless garden appraisals that include words such as 'peace' and 'heaven'. As if to confirm the various appraisals there is a part of Glendurgan known as the Holy Corner, or Heavenly Bank, which features trees such as the Judas tree, *Cercis siliquastrum*, the tree of heaven, *Ailanthus altissima*, two types of the tree of the crown of thorns, *Colletia paradoxa* (syn. *C. cruciata*), and *Poncirus trifoliata*, and the Glastonbury thorn, *Crataegus monogyna* 'Biflora'. Planting in threes as a symbol of the Holy Trinity was also popular, and often looks better than single planting.

Colletia paradoxa

Because the gift of nature was perceived to be entirely by grace, and essential for our survival, and because life in itself is a gift, the Quakers were very aware of the concept of stewardship. George Fox, the founder of Quakerism, and other Quakers since have attached considerable importance to the educative value of plants. No doubt the garden at La Mortola in northern Italy receives accolades similar to those received by Glendurgan: it too was the inspiration of a Quaker family, the Hanburys. With its steep geography and views of the sea there is some parallel with Glendurgan. In terms of plants, La Mortola has a strong working relationship with another Cornish garden, Tresco, in the Isles of Scilly.

The following entry from Alfred's son George's diary for 23 August 1923 describes a dialogue between two of his sisters. It shows that Rachel, who was living at Glendurgan, seemed to have a reluctance to leave this Heaven on Earth:

RET had a strong desire to live as long as possible and when Lucy said to her lately how she envied her coming so near to the gates of Heaven RET burst out 'THAT is just what I want to avoid.'

In their search for a Heaven on Earth, Quakers tend to take a benevolent attitude towards their fellow men, and to say, or see, or do good wherever they can. Elton Fox, a grandson of George Fox, records that at a certain wedding party 'everyone conversed for two hours in low tones discretion watchful', which must have been frustrating to a degree, 'against any happy lapse into the unprofitable', that is, into gossiping. At other times their positive attitude must have been rather surprising. Cholera raging in Falmouth did not deter Alfred Fox from planting the maze. Perhaps he was not aware of the original meaning of a maze being described as 'a series of irregular winding walks that remind us of life, where we may go wrong in a multitude of ways, but right only in one'.

In 1837 Alfred burst out laughing when he heard that his thatched cottage had burnt to the ground. The apparent disaster solved a problem that he was in the midst of discussing: the accommodation of his ever-increasing family. Such a response was perhaps a reason for his son George later to write, 'He avoided controversy and was bright and cheery and submissive even to bad treatment'.

George's own sense of priorities was clear: family and fruit-growing were of more immediate importance than the state of the nation. Thus he wrote in 1914, 'Romney shot his first rabbit – war matters very disturbing – apples are very prolific this season and an extraordinary size'. One of his grandchildren, on hearing of the transfer of ownership of Glendurgan to the National Trust, and of consequent mutterings about the admittance of the public, could only say, 'Oh at last – how wonderful that it can now be shared'. She probably meant the general public, although from time to time the garden was, and still is, open for specific charities. But what equally she may have been envisaging was a return to the sort of place she had known as a child, always full of visitors. My own father will not countenance bad news. When trees have come down he will immediately think of replacements, and once when the office staff were preoccupied at work with the aftermath of a fairly serious burglary, his response was, 'It's low tide and I'm off prawning.'

These worthy attributes do not deny the fact that the Foxes had their human frailties and susceptibilities as much as anyone else. They were not immune to romance. There was a time, up to 1860, when Quakers could marry only within their own sect. As is so clearly detected in her journals this must have been a source of tension for Caroline Fox, who was an intellectual and close friend to many of the handsome, but not Quaker, lions of literature of the last century, and in particular John Sterling. It must have been a double-edged token that she was also very intelligent: she could see the ludicrous side of her predicament, yet was able to cope with it. In the later years of her life as a spinster it almost seemed as if the energy she had for forming relationships outside her circle became redirected towards charitable work, although she did indeed come from a genuinely philanthropic background. For others who did not share this frustration there were all the usual restraints that one would expect in an average Victorian family of Quaker descent. It was that background, also possibly an acquaintance with Penjerrick or Glendurgan, which may have inspired a Penjerrick connection, Herbert Trench, to write the following lines, included here because they are so descriptive of the romantic nature of the garden, and also the sense of benison which so many have experienced therein:

> O dreamy, gloomy, friendly Trees,
> I came along your narrow track
> To bring my gifts unto your knees
> And gifts did you give back;
> For when I brought this heart that burns –
> These thoughts that bitterly repine –
> And laid them here among the ferns
> And the hum of boughs divine,
> Ye, vastest breathers of the air,
> Shook down with slow and mighty poise
> Your coolness on the human care,
> Your wonder on its toys,
> Your greenness on the heart's despair,
> Your darkness on its noise.

Tulip trees, 'vastest breathers of the air'

However, not all was despair. George had a daughter who successfully prosecuted her relationship with a local farmer by arranging a secret place in the bough of a secret tree for the secret exchange of secret letters. My great-grandmother, George's wife Rachel, confined to a bath chair, is reported to have said to a potential daughter-in-law, 'I never leave the terrace these days', only to be seen 20 minutes later by her son and his intended wife whizzing along, dissuasively but to no avail, behind some trees in the Camellia Walk. On another occasion she was more successful, when on returning from Durgan one summer's evening, she was surprised by the incongruous sight of two pairs of clothed legs, 'a man's and a woman's' (at least she could be thankful for that), poking out from under some bushes; mercifully, as she went on to discover, neither belonging to any member of her family, present or future. The offenders 'pretended they did not know it was private property', which, although demonstrating naivety to Rachel, may have seemed of little relevance.

Trebah

Family group at Glendurgan

The humble origins of Glendurgan are very much part of its Quaker character. The original cottage and garden were not bought as a complete estate, but were acquired over a number of years as different plots of land, mostly orchards. Some of the names such as Manderson's Hill and Birch's Orchard are still in use, although there is now no trace of the fruit trees that once grew there. In 1893, in a land tax appeal, George did explain that originally the land had in fact been part of Trebah estate, which at one time had been the property of the Bishop of Exeter; and to the east of Glendurgan the next large estate was Trerose.

To digress, for a moment, into the origins of the other two Fox gardens, Charles Fox's tenancy of Trebah from the Nicholls family began in 1830–1831, and he bought it in 1838. Unlike Glendurgan, the house was then already *in situ* at the head of wooded valley. It was considerably enlarged between 1856 and 1857, ultimately having five sitting rooms on the ground floor and one upstairs. Compared with Glendurgan, Trebah had become, for Cornwall, a moderately grand house. Sadly, as at Glendurgan, Trebah also fell victim to fire, in 1948, leaving the existing house of 1760, with its twentieth-century extension to the west. Fire was a common fate of houses lit by oil lamps and candles, and heated with open grates.

The earliest reference to the Fox family at Penjerrick is in papers dated 1765, when it was leased as a farm to the first George Croker Fox of Grove Hill House. Later, in 1838, it came into the hands of his grandson Robert Were Fox, who with his son Barclay created the garden.

In all three gardens the indigenous trees, the glades of grass, and banks of wild flowers are as crucial as the great horticultural species, not only in their own right, but also in the way in which they combine like ingredients in a recipe. Glendurgan would diminish without its banks of columbines, as would

Penjerrick without its fritillaries, and Tre-bah without its slopes of falling daffodils. Sometimes it seems that the cultivated species complement the wild flowers in much the same way as the hound complements the terrier in Landseer's famous painting, *Dignity and Impudence*. A *Magnolia denudata*, for example, will highlight a nearby carpet of wood anenomes, and the palm *Trachycarpus fortunei* will hold up honey-suckle in the fingers of its leaves.

Glendurgan has evolved from the Quaker inclination towards simplicity, functionalism, and the more Shaker belief that if something operates well it will inevitably look aesthetically pleasing – it is not surprising that there have always been Quakers on the peripheries of the

Primroses, violets and celandines with *Magnolia denudata*

Acquilegia

art world. An example of this is the continuing use of beach cobbles by the National Trust on a steep section of path where the size and shape of the cobbles are complemented by the leaves of the bordering *Rhododendron yakushimanum*, and elsewhere in the creation of gullies and drainage channels. In general, paths and drives are designed not only to be practical on so many inclines, but also to be pleasing to so many eyes.

Both George and his father wisely followed the local tradition of growing fruit. In Alfred's time, it was not long before a substantial wall was built to the north-west of the house, giving shelter to the most vulnerable area of what was to become the walled garden. Although brick was known to be a better conductor of heat, stone was used for this wall. Whether this represented a Quaker economy in such a mild climate,

Rhododendron augustinii and wood anemones

Rhododendron yakushimanum

or lack of resources, or merely ignorance, is unknown. The seriously affluent, such as Sir Rose Price at Trengwainton, near Penzance, selected brick, while the really clever, as so wonderfully illustrated at Heligan, at Pentewan, built the lower half of their walls with stone and the upper half, where warmth was required, with brick.

Trengwainton

From early primitive pictures showing rows of produce being harvested, it is easy to imagine the original character of Glendurgan. George's diaries substantiate that part of the garden's venture was the sale of produce, especially fruit. In 1926 an ash and an elm tree were felled, and found their way to the family's timber yard at Fox Stanton; nothing of commercial value was wasted. Elton Fox described the prodigious nature of the garden:

The walled garden stands back from the drive from house to stables.
Fruit trees all along the walls, peaches and nectarines and citrons,
the latter covered with glass. Rows of pear trees follow and line the
paths. Orange trees provide blossoms for family weddings.

Beehives were introduced, and ponds were dug and stocked with trout. From Alfred's journal, an entry for 1830 reads:

I put 57 trout into the new pond – the first fish placed there – on the
13th. I caught 62 more trout at Manaccan, and on the 20th 142 more
– all to be put in the new pond.'

With a family of 12 children, and maintaining Glendurgan as a second home, it was essential that the garden should be able to run itself on productive and self-sustaining lines. Alfred, it is said, 'could enthuse over the first appearance of ducks and green peas or strawberries and cream'.

Many modern gardeners like to have two of everything in the tool shed. In former times it was different: without any of the machinery of today, and none of its bureaucracy, every single thing had its own place and purpose. Husbandry was as paramount at Glendurgan as at any estate. The donkeys that pulled the cart laden with seaweed for compost would also don leather clogs to help to cut the grass. It is probably thanks to the habits of the donkey, and to banks too steep for tractors, that Glendurgan has been able to maintain a rare example of unadulterated grassland, rich in interest both botanically and biologically.

Anchor chain, presumably obtained through contacts in the shipping world, was used in 1898 and 1899 to edge the lane which runs down to Durgan. A section of the chain was examined in Falmouth docks, which revealed that it contained a high percentage of pure iron, possibly obtained from Sweden.

The wrought-iron gate to the walled garden (which is in private use) survived during times of war due to the diligence of my grandfather who thoughtfully had it interred in the woods. Contributing towards the well-being of the garden there were a number of functional components: the water pumps, apple sheds, stick shed, paint shed, linhay, cloches, cold frames, fruit cages, and greenhouses.

For a family that attached such importance to the careful management of their affairs and, at Glendurgan, self-sufficiency, it must have been gruelling to have had to pay tithes to a denomination to which they did not belong.

Quakers believed that ministry was God-given and should not be paid for, or rewarded. They objected to paying taxes because they objected to money being spent on armaments and conflict. George wrote that his father, being a true Quaker,

> refused consistently to pay Rector's Rate Tithes, Fish Tithes etc & Wodehouse Place was repeatedly stripped of furniture & silver to meet same. Fish tithes at Mevagissey & elsewhere were peculiarly unjust & obnoxious, & the cause of much heart burning. At Glendurgan the carts & pigs were taken, & the pony was threatened: but in later days it was generally coals & sometimes William Rogers the Clerk got it from the coal merchant who sent in the bill for the coals without the coals ever being delivered to Glendurgan.
>
> It is said that a certain Shoemaker in Falmouth objected to pay the Rector's rate & the Rector called on him, and argued the matter, & said seats were available for the Shoemaker & his family in the church – & the Shoemaker said he did not want the seats, & the Rector replied "but you might have them". The Rector ordered a pair of boots & at the end of the year the S'maker sent a bill for two pair of boots & the Rector called on him, & said he had not had two pairs. The Shoemaker replied 'True, but you might have had them'.

Although the habit of other nineteenth-century families, it was especially so with some of the more committed Quakers that their unshakeable belief in God permeated every aspect of their lives, including their businesses. Within the family's archives there is from that time hardly a letter that does not contain a lengthy preamble of meditative Christian thought. Here is an extract from a letter to Alfred from his daughter Lucy. It illustrates the depth and sincerity of Quakers, and also their attitude to possessions:

> Last night I had a very vivid dream of thee and Mamma. We were all sitting together after an evening reading and you both exhorted us very beautifully and earnestly to leave the vanities that beset us so closely in this world and to find all our pleasures in Christ and in following Him closely – Most of your children were present and many of us were touched to tears and (I) woke up sobbing with a sense of my short comings – but some voice I can't tell whose said 'We may not sorrow as those without hope for we are accepted in Christ'.

Alfred wrote in his journal, one of many prayerful entries centred on the nature of repentance, forgiveness, and redemption:

> May I more earnestly seek for a place of deep repentance and contrition of heart to be humbled in the very dust and to be able to ask for forgiveness of God through and for the sake of my crucified Redeemer. I have learnt this sad lesson, and I cannot trust myself for any one thing. I can indeed speak of marvellous loving kindness and forbearance.

No doubt it was a struggle reconciling all his blessings with the thorny path of faith – his niece Mariana Tuckett once confessed her 'sin in ordering chops for tea'.

An early Quaker plant collector, John Bartram, had inscribed over the door of his greenhouse 'looks through nature up to nature's God'. In line with his sentiments are the memoirs of one of Alfred's grandchildren, Ellen Bosanquet. Subjectively, she linked her awareness of nature to the general creed, and her love of nature to her love of God:

> I believe in God, Maker of Heaven and earth, of all things visible and invisible. As long as I can remember I have loved Him because of the beauty which I see and the order from which I believe it springs. When evil has shown its ugliest face I can still look at any flower and feel the God who made it.

From the countless references in her uncle George's diaries it can be inferred that he experienced the same blessing from his appreciation of garden birds, and from their appreciation of him and his crumb-laden pockets. He must have reminded many of his uncle Joshua, not often given a mention, but remarkable for his unity with all things natural, and for his spirituality. John Harris immortalizes him as follows:

Joshua Fox

> Here dwells, amid the laurel green,
> The genius of this tranquil scene,
> Beneath the boughs of evergreen
> His spirit worships the UNSEEN (sic)

Cousin Nellie, as she was known, continued:

> I believe in the Holy Spirit, Lord and Giver of Life. These magnanimous life-giving powers now manifested all around me in this exquisite spring world whose beauty sometimes lifts the curtain of sense, so that we can see spirits Holy and profane still continuing that battle of light against darkness… I believe in one Baptism for the Remission of Sins… I only remember feeling broken by the beauty of earth and sky – so broken that I fell on my knees.

Her kind of prayer entry does not exclude the sentiments of Alfred. It is rather the change in emphasis which is interesting, as is the lamentable fact that for so many the emphasis has nowadays become one further step removed: flora and fauna are pursued for their own sake without any reference to a God of creation, genius and design. Ironically, there seems to be a resurgence of interest by garden designers today in the eighteenth-century concept of 'spirit of place'.

It is an encouraging development that a relatively modern practice, within Christian circles, known as 'open prayer' is totally Quaker in concept: prayers are dependent upon the movement and inspiration of the Holy Spirit in one's being. Indeed, it is said of George Fox, the founder of Quakerism, that he discovered 'in his own spirit the place where a seed of Divine life was springing up, the place where the voice of a Divine teacher was being uttered, the place that was being inhabited by a Divine and glorious presence'. Because this was the essence of the Quaker life, and something that pervaded every other part, here is a description of a Quaker meeting, much the same as any prayer group. It is written by one of Alfred's grandchildren:

> We would collect in the drawing-room and sit gravely in a circle. The solemnity of the occasion gradually sank over us. The conversation slowly drooped and drooped and died away almost imperceptibly. We strove – at least I hope we strove – to let our thoughts be 'gathered' (a favourite Quaker word) as we lapsed into silence – a long silence, broken at last when the Friend, waiting on Divine Guidance in perfect surrender, might offer prayer, or perhaps quietly lift up his or her voice – often broken by a tender hesitation – to give utterance to an outpouring of the Holy Spirit. No sermon this. There was nothing set or conventionally eloquent about the Address, and yet the simple, unpremeditated words were far more solemn and soul-moving than any mere religious talk could ever be; for they were spoken trembling under the weight of the Message.

With Quaker tendencies, there have always been many family members who prayed both for their descendants and for the future of their homes. On 7 August 1911 George records: 'lovely people on a lovely day in a lovely place… all men in drawing-room 91st psalm… a strong prayer from Violet, a few words from RJF… peace perfect peace sang… Lily playing'. Such is the pattern of prayerfulness, and it comes as no surprise that in recent years baptisms have been held off Durgan beach. I myself have had a dream in which there was, just below the bamboo bridge, a small pool in which people were being baptized. Without describing the location, I narrated this dream to some friends from our church. They walked around the entire garden and then stopped on the bamboo bridge, and said 'It's here isn't it?' Subsequently a four-year-old boy visiting the garden surprised his parents by putting his hands together at this exact spot and praying, 'Thank you God for giving us this beautiful garden' – words which underline the *raison d' être* for this particular chapter.

CHILDREN
CHAPTER FOUR

Celebrations at Durgan
'Mr Pease has lately bought a large portion of Durgan village, with the
adjoining estate of Bosveal, and after pulling down and rebuilding most
of the old cottages, and making many additions, and sanitary and other
improvements, he completed his alterations by removing the old fish cellar,
in the loft of which a school for some years had been carried on. Mr Pease has
built on this site a beautiful and capacious schoolroom, which was formally
opened by him yesterday, when the children of the village and neighbourhood,
their parents and many friends, enjoyed an excellent tea. The villagers had
prepared a welcome for Mr Pease by decorating their village on both sides of
the valley profusely with flags, evergreens, arches, and mottoes, while from
nearly every fisherman's boat gay flags were flying. Mr Pease arrived at
Durgan in his steam launch Rosebery, which was also completely dressed in
bright bunting, and she greatly added to the scene.

(Life in Cornwall 1876)

Durgan: The Schoolroom, with nets hanging over the wall

Sarah Fox

The cider press

Alfred's nieces, Caroline and Anna Maria, founded the Royal Cornwall Polytechnic Society in 1833 for the education of the underprivileged. Members of the family lectured there on subjects ranging from mackerel to mining. Having a large family, Sarah Fox, Alfred's wife, must have been acutely aware of the value of education. She might also have felt privileged to have been in a position to educate children; it was very much part of any Quaker, as well as Victorian, upbringing to exercise the brain. It would therefore have been a natural step coming from such a background, steeped in philanthropy, to start in 1829 the first school in Mawnan Smith. As Alfred said, it became 'the object of her care'. It was run in the woods at the end of what has become known as the Schoolroom Walk, until the summer of 1842 when it closed, and subsequently became a cider-house: the cider press is there to see today.

Sarah mused sorrowfully:

After return to Wodehouse Place after two months at the cottage it seems truly reposeful to have my principal duties and interests brought into a narrower focus, narrower however in one respect than I anticipated or wished having closed the school at Glendurgan which for near 14 years has claimed my unremitting care. Several circumstances lead to this somewhat hasty step, but I do not doubt it being a right one painful as it has been to me and almost mournful.

It was a sad and difficult decision, but one that led perhaps to her son-in-law, Joseph Pease, building a proper schoolhouse in Durgan in 1876. This became in time a reading room, where men from the village could gather, and as from about 1930 children could also be admitted when outside play was rendered impossible by foul weather. As children we used to play with a seesaw – a vestige from this era: George had it installed on the schoolroom quay for the use of the local children.

In the 1950s we grew up in the knowledge, to begin with subconscious, that our lives were slightly different from those of anyone who lived the other side of the River Tamar. Everything was related to the fact that on three sides of Cornwall we were surrounded by sea. Our walks were always down to the beach, and having arrived there we would stand and watch the sea abstractedly, like people who walk to the end of the pier. The walls in our house were dominated by pictures of boats, and some pictures of only sea. In a room known as 'the cloaks' there was an assortment of strange-looking clothes: heavy, salt-stained oilskins and sou'westers. We went sailing, which usually meant lying for a very long time among a pile of sails in the forecastle. But our connections with the sea went beyond recreational activities. Glendurgan is not far as the crow flies, and as does the helicopter, from the Royal Naval Air Station at Culdrose. By day we waved optimistically at passing helicopters, and at night we raced out of bed to watch their twinkling lights. Sometimes we heard that our father had been on a ship in the night, but we never really knew why. During the week he went to a place that was called the office, which with much trepidation we occasionally visited. It was a noisy, dark place, and full of old men who smoked, and who patted our shoulders, and gave us ice-creams. Sometimes he returned from the office with, to a child, terrifyingly important-looking captains in full regalia. It was never explained, but I knew that all these influences, all this conditioning, were part of something very big and important that had to do with ships and grown-ups, and safety and danger. Against this background I painted my canvas with plants – and in later life it was against a similar background of working in the family ship agency that I became a garden designer.

D.M. Thomas, in a lyrical poem on Glendurgan, describes Durgan thus:

I should remember Durgan
I was taken here as a child
many times, and the word 'Durgan' brought joy to my parents eyes;
but coming here today, carrying
a child in my arms, I can recognise
nothing of this enchanted
estuary. I can remember only
a flash of pebbles, and being carried
in someone's arms

Bosahan

To me as a child, after emerging from the relative coolness of the garden, Durgan was a place of vivid colours and aridity, of fuchsias and geraniums, of boats and sails, of stones and shells, and of smells – those of rotting fish, and some kind of pitch boiled up to preserve the nets, which were then left out to dry. It was also a place of sounds, close by those of budgerigars and doves; and across the water, from the towers of old Bosahan, that of the clock chiming, or the church bell of St Anthony; or out to sea the foghorn on a foggy day, and around the corner from the Nare at Porthoustock, the stone quarries being blasted. Some of these sounds drifted up the valley and into our lives, symbols of time and of calling, of guidance and action; and early in the morning or late at night nothing challenged the imagination more than the *putt-putt-putt* sound of an inboard engine.

But what made Durgan most colourful were the inhabitants, most of whom never seemed to come out of their cottages. The women stood there at their half-open stable doors, happily concealing the effects of an operation my great uncle asserted was performed on cottage-dwellers in order to fit them into their low accommodation. Coming from a tallish family, for a long time I had a fear of a *tibioctomy*.

Alfred Fox sired one child for each month of the year, 'a good beginning', as a friend said to him. The character of the house was probably that of what could be called a beach house, where the atmosphere is informal, and children would have been crammed into dormitories or attics. That was of no matter: they were there for the garden.

All the Fox gardens abound with areas to explore, and which lend themselves to imaginative pursuits. A cousin wrote of Glendurgan:

[we] discovered in the pathless woods, among seas of garlic, a
disused old ciderhouse. Here we had glorious plays of Cavaliers and
Roundheads. The smell of wood smoke or trampled garlic always
recalls mixed feelings of guilt and glory.

A playground for children was described at Penjerrick by the *Gardener's Chronicle* in 1874: 'It is this view of a species of fairyland which has made the reputation of Penjerrick; it will certainly repay a journey of many hundred miles for a glimpse of this view alone'. In 1897 Hamilton Davey, in the *Journal of the Royal Institute of Cornwall*, wrote:

At Penjerrick, which every Cornishman knows as a bit of the tropics
come up for an airing – the judicious introduction of an exotic
flora has produced a scene as ravishing and romantic as any bit of
fairyland. If anywhere in Cornwall, it is here that the wizardry and
abandon of nature are felt to the full.

In 1899 he made further allusions to fairyland when he wrote that, 'at Penjerrick [a] magic wand of love and skill brought gardening near perfection'. So it was that many childhoods were lived out against this background of enchanted gardens.

I recollect the feeling of guilt, usually after the event, although sometimes it would be before, as when inviting the unwary visitor to sample the delicious-looking, but inedible, fruits of the strawberry tree *Arbutus unedo*, or of

Cornus kousa

Cornus kousa var. *chinensis*. Mostly our activities as children were harmless, such as running along and jumping off roofs and walls, climbing trees and turning them into ships, diverting and damming streams, hiding nettles and frogs in the gardeners' gumboots, and watching sparks fly as we operated the knife sharpener in their potting shed.

One of the worst things we ever did was to encourage a reluctant bonfire by pouring on to it a can of petrol from the garage. Seconds later the nearby tent caught fire, parted from its guy ropes and took off breezily across the lawn, with my brother Robert and me in what we quickly understood to be known as hot pursuit. My mother had a reasonable view of this escapade from an upstairs window, out of which she happened to be shaking a duster at the time.

Much more serious was another occasion when, as a surprise for my grandmother, I picked several hundred red tulips, all neatly severed just below the head. Regrettably no one had mentioned that on the next day the garden was due to be opened in aid of the Red Cross (charity openings were very much part of its use). Well might she have become both red and cross, but her reaction was one of silence – out of shock or wisdom I shall never know. Generally people were more frightened of her than they needed to be, but I still quake at the memory of her legs the other side of a raspberry cane I was once secretly stripping of fruit. I cannot imagine how I ever fell into that unfortunate predicament, for she had a built-in early warning signal, in the form of a repetitive cough by which, with unlimited appreciation for some, her whereabouts could be easily pinpointed.

As a boy, George, her father-in-law, had often found himself in far more serious trouble:

Agave americana, 2004

I was the worst of the family for stealing fruit and good things from the pantry, and on one occasion was sent to my bed in the night nursery and probably at Mother's instigation Father came up with a horse whip, and told me I must be whipped for it. Before beginning he said, 'Tell me when thee have had enough', and after the first cut I sang out so lustily there was no mistaking my opinion – and it was the only occasion any of us was whipped as far as I know.

Less physical but perhaps more terrifying were the threats of my grandfather who one day caught a small boy using a penknife to carve his name into the leaf of an *Agave americana*: when the sap has dried any inscription becomes quite legible. 'Roll up your sleeve,' he said, 'perhaps you would like to know what it feels like.' I cannot recall that he had any dissuasive procedure for the boy who is drawn irresistibly to putting his fingers into the tentacles of a sea anemone.

No child visiting the house – privately occupied – has ever been able to resist climbing the early eighteenth-century moorstone lions that lie at each end of the terrace. Originally these stood guard outside George Croker Fox's Bank House in Falmouth. In 1788 his son, the second George Croker, built Grove Hill House, leaving his surgeon brother Joseph Fox at Bank House. His son, another Joseph, also went into the medical world, finally retiring in 1800 to a house called Wood Cottage, now known as Greatwood, on a promontory between Mylor and Restronguet. This property, which predated Glendurgan, must have been beloved by children, for according to the Cornish historian Charles Gilbert:

> The situation and embellishments of this charming retreat render it a place of uncommon interest. The moss-house, walks, and resting seats, are constructed with that superior taste, and philosophic arrangement, which give a varied beauty to the multiplicity of objects which nature and art have assembled together. The avenues, which open through the woods, let in a diversity of pleasing objects, romantically situated on the juts of Falmouth Harbour; and the variety of trading vessels which are constantly coasting up and down the river… give it an air of gaiety and general cheerfulness.

One of these 'pleasing objects', so history revealed, was to be a granite lion, which came from Bank House, presumably floated across the harbour. Joseph must have been a keen gardener because an advertisement in the *Royal Cornwall Gazette* of 1805 reads as follows:

> Wanted by a regular retired family in the country, a confidential man servant. His time will seldom be required in the house, as his superintendence and assistance will be required to keep the Garden, Grounds and a small farm (together only fourteen acres) in neat order, with a labourer and a boy. Apply to Doctor Fox, Wood Cottage, Mylor.

By 1979 the garden at Greatwood was far from being neat, for it was in that year that underneath a mass of brambles in the derelict kitchen garden a friend of the family, Ann Le Grice, came across a granite lion. She alerted the then Regional Director of the National Trust, Michael Trinick, who a few years previously had written an article in the *Journal of the Royal Institution of Cornwall* about the Arundell granite lions, now the property of the National Trust at Trerice. As a tail-piece he mentioned the granite lion that my grandfather had brought out from Bank House to Glendurgan in 1946, in the hope that its brother would one day materialize – which is exactly what then

The Lion.
Bank House Hotel.
Falmouth.

Frank Atherley, Michael Holland-Hibbert, Philip Fox, Michael Trinick and John Milan with the new lion

Its twin

happened. The owners and restorers of Great-wood House, Frank Atherley and John Milan, gave the second lion to the National Trust, and in 1980 the pair was reunited, the face of the Greatwood one distinctly less weathered from its years in the undergrowth than the face of the Glendurgan one.

As a footnote, for some of the intervening years Greatwood was owned by the Dorrien-Smiths of Tresco, a garden which is rich in statuary. Floating several tons of granite lion from Mylor to the Scillies was obviously for them, in spite of their well-attested seamanship, not an option.

Activities were not limited to the garden. Barclay Fox wrote:

> to most of the visiting cousins Glendurgan was looked upon as the prime summer haunt for boating bathing fishing and picnics… Off we set in two boats and came to an anchor about a mile beyond the Manacles. We lit a fire and having taken tea we commenced operations; the evening was delightful. The bright fire with the men lying smoking round it and the clear moon shining on the rigging made the scene very picturesque.

In the world beyond the garden were the fields of Trebah and the jungly woods of Carwinion, the home of an eccentric cousin, his housekeeper and cat, both also eccentric. Often these places had a far greater attraction than the forms of recreation within Glendurgan. But the seriously alluring 'undiscovered territory' was the Nare. Like a distant wreck out at sea this headland is visible from the public car-park, and from other places in the garden, but always and romantically through a veil of trees. Elton Fox wrote, beautifully:

> the real romance of the river hung over the distant Nare. We never
> went there though we always longed to go. Low, fern-grown,
> deserted, it stretches a remote, grey finger far out to sea. That dim
> shore only broken by solitary beaches, seemed a no-man's-land, the
> very port for exploration. Men may come and settle and civilise the
> opposite coast, but for ten thousand years it can have known no
> change. And when caught in the last gleam of sunset lingering there
> after the river and its enveloping hills have been lost in a shadow, the
> lonely headland becomes the Land's End of a world more primitive
> – more legendary and mysterious than our own.

With a beloved English setter as an inexhaustible companion, I used to walk for miles along the coast, captivated by the composition formed by headlands and woodlands descending into gentian seas. It was intoxicating, and on returning home at the end of a four-hour walk we would go off again. Sometimes during the summer I would get up at 5 or 6 a.m. and dip down into a still shady but awakening valley, and then out on to the headlands as they began to be hit by the first fingers of sun. Once, on the brow of a hill, I was sitting on a stile and seven swans flew over my head, inches away. I walked on and came across a large family of foxes at play. For both the animal and the man there was no more beautiful place in which to be raised.

This was in spite of the fact that, like so many English families, we were living in post-war austerity and surviving on a regime of no central heating, very sensible English food, and a succession of thick red jerseys which could be spotted easily if we were lost or in trouble. We would have to ask permission to 'play' the wireless, let alone the television. As for a refrigerator, amazingly at Glendurgan there was one, which produced only small, finger-size rectangles of the most delicious vanilla ice cream, whereas the refrigerator at Trebah did better with a small supply of lollipops, much to our delight, but to our mother's dismay. The people next door also owned a navy blue 'Jag', which added an extra dimension to our occasional expeditions, and compared favourably with our world of half-timbered Morris Traveller vans and twin-toned Wolseleys. In this respect there was my mother's faint surprise at anything bordering on the luxurious, and in marked contrast to the trends of today, her disapproval of any display of financial expenditure. Again in contrast to the consumer-orientated childhoods of today, we passed much of our time mooching around. Once in the summer I caught my younger brother, William, mesmerized by a dragonfly hovering over a water lily – Glendurgan is an insect's, and an

insect lover's paradise. 'What are you doing?' I questioned. 'Oh just aestivating,' came with a smile the reply, his apposite word for the opposite of hibernating.

In the centre of the garden lies, delight-fully terrifying for a child, the maze. To lose one's friends in it was, is, and always will be the greatest fun. In its history, however, it does seem to have had other purposes. Eliza-beth Tuckett in her diary of 1854 wrote: 'we dined in the house and then lay on the grass and sang until we joined the gentlemen who had retired to the labyrinth to smoke. We sat in the arbour there for some time and then returned to the house for tea.'

Along the Schoolroom Walk stands a may-pole, endearingly referred to in a child's poem as follows: 'There is a rocky hill that leads to/A maple straight and still… .' It became known as the Giant Stride, erected in 1913 on a site formerly occupied by what might have been called, in contrast, the dwarf croquet ground. It was so small that baby mallets had to be used.

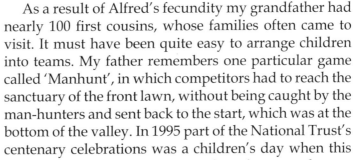

As a result of Alfred's fecundity my grandfather had nearly 100 first cousins, whose families often came to visit. It must have been quite easy to arrange children into teams. My father remembers one particular game called 'Manhunt', in which competitors had to reach the sanctuary of the front lawn, without being caught by the man-hunters and sent back to the start, which was at the bottom of the valley. In 1995 part of the National Trust's centenary celebrations was a children's day when this game was resurrected, and renamed more amicably and aptly 'Foxes and Badgers' – for years the Fox family and the Badger family have enjoyed living respectively at the top and bottom of the valley. Another energetic pursuit was to work out the maximum combination of strength and speed in order to collect the heaviest load of stones from Durgan beach, and be the first to dump them at the foot of the tulip trees. It took a long time for them to be removed – a change to the normal run of tasks performed by the gardeners, for whose workload children held scant regard.

There was also a non-migratory population of cousins, some of whom were alive in the middle of the nineteenth century, as well as in the twentieth. These were members of the Society of Friends, devout Quakers and worthy of respect. A few of the ladies were so frail, my brother Robert cheerfully informed me one day, that they had to wear the cameo-bearing black velvet ribbons around their necks in order to prevent their heads from wobbling off on to the ground. Even more miraculously, the ornate hatpins which prevented their bonnets from blowing off in the wind achieved their purpose by actually being inserted, fakir style, through the back of the head. Along with crocodiles in the pond, and tigers in the bamboos, these snippets of knowledge were added to my fast-growing list of very useful information.

FAMILY DUTY
THE SECOND GENERATION
CHAPTER FIVE

*'The loveliness and interest attached to the spot for old
associations invest it with a charm to my mind far beyond
any pecuniary advantages I can hope to reap from it.'*

(Barclay Fox, 19 March 1837, on acquiring Penjerrick)

Alfred died in 1874, and his widow Sarah followed on Christmas Eve 1890. In
February 1891, by arrangement with his brothers Theodore, Howard, and Wilson, Glendurgan was bought by George. The estate was then let, in particular
to George's sister Rachel Tuckett. George's interest in the place, however, was
not undiminished, and in 1912 he decided to build

View from apple shed across to Helford

a hut for apples and room for afternoon tea facing Helford
River. Cuthbert designed it and Harry Rashleigh put it
up, with some alteration to C.'s design which included a
verandah… Debell Tuckett had kindly sent suggestions of
G. Bunyard and Son Maidstone as to best sort of apple room
– thatched roof etc. Wm Eddy advised shelf arrangements
etc. – no reed being obtainable till after harvest a wooden
temporary roof was put on till Sept – Oct when Geo Pascoe
of Bones Mill Hill thatched it – Wm and Peter Eddy cut
the paths thro' the larches to road over cliff and to Grebe
orchard. It proved a good apple room – and it was a good
season of apples most of which Peter gathered. G. H. Fox
thinning them when young and helping to bag some of the
finest in muslin bags to prevent blackbirds tits robins etc
attacking the fruit.

This tiny building, enshrined by pines, is now a holiday-let with
glorious views south-west up the river. It was visited frequently
by George's family and their friends, and they preferred its modesty to the house at Glendurgan. A note dating from February
1922 shows the role that it played as a second or recreational
home, and the humble attitude that the family had towards its
use:

I generally of a Sunday post a p.c. to Mrs Tresise to say which
day we are coming out in that week and to order milk
etc. Geo Retallack (blind) who fetches the milk – with her
consent – asks the post girl if there is a p.c. for Mrs T. from
me and if so gets her to read it to him so he learns our needs,
and conveniently.

Mr Retallack was also relied upon by the local fisher-men: living in Durgan he learned to tell when Spring and Neap tides were due, in addition to the times of high and low water. As with the previous extract from George's journal, there is a sense of the local community being involved with the activities of the family, in a way that might not be expected. Individuals who worked for the family were mentioned by name and with respect.

In 1920 many of the villagers from Mawnan Smith and from Durgan attended a party being given in hon-our of the marriage of one of George's daughters, Erica. It was held in Falmouth at Wodehouse Place, which most of the guests had never before visited, although, 'they had for many years been familiar with the back door bringing fish etc for sale'. George expressed 'plea-sure at the good muster', but the most revealing remark came from one of the revellers: 'I wouldn't have missed it for 10/-; how can you like stopping at Durgan with such a lovely great house of your own?' It is a signifi-cant part of Glendurgan's history that it represented, in concept, and for decades in practice, a way of life which differed from the formalities of Falmouth. Many of the family have continued to enjoy the simple pleasures of village life in Durgan, not least of which is being always within earshot of the sounds of the sea.

This compares dramatically with what was going on at Trebah. Charles Fox had died in 1878, and the prop-erty had passed to his son-in-law Edmund Backhouse, MP for Darlington, then to his son Jonathan. Edmund had been a colourful individual who became one of the last courtiers to the Empress of China, and about whom Hugh Trevor-Roper wrote a biography called *Hermit of Peking*. That would have pleased Charles, who was a keen sinologist as well as being an avid reader. Then for a time Trebah was home to the Hexts, who introduced flamingoes to the lake at the bottom of the garden, and who in 1935 acted as hosts to Ernest and Wallis Simp-son, with the Prince of Wales in tow, as had the Foxes at Penjerrick. The Prince was later to receive a consignment of Trebah plants for his garden at The Fort in Sunning-dale. Later, at some point, Trebah belonged to the Healeys of Austin Healey Sprite fame. They were responsible for adding to the exotic allure of the prop-

Rhododendrons Trebah Gem, Cornish Cross and Penjerrick at Trebah, by Miss Beatrice Parsons, 1924

erty by installing closed-circuit television, and miles of protective fencing. They also tidied up the beach by removing its wartime concrete apron. Eventually Trebah passed to Major and Mrs Hibbert, who created the Trebah Garden Trust, in order to ensure the garden's preservation for ever. The history of Trebah is in these ways more colourful than that of Glendurgan, and the Trebah Garden Trust has successfully enhanced this with a wealth of sub-tropical plants and an exotic water garden. This is crowned by a gazebo, and further up the slope is situated a pool for the pleasurable existence of some Koi carp. The spirit of entrepreneurialism and innovation continues with the installation in 2003 of a conference centre.

Koi carp pool, Trebah

Glendurgan in part took shape by virtue of the fact that Alfred and George were prepared to put their hands to the plough. They were, of course, supported by proficient and dedicated head gardeners: there are copious references in particular to William Eddy, who worked at Glendurgan for over 50 years. But no task was too mean or too lowly for any member of the family. Alfred did not employ an apiarist, but dealt with the hives himself; and even if he had, he would have treated him as an equal – Barclay Fox from Penjerrick used to have Christmas dinner with one of his faithful servants.

The Foxes expected and received willing and active participation from their wives and children. 'My boys and I cut down trees at Glendurgan,' reported Alfred in 1847. Sarah was also a great clearer as well as planter of trees. In 1897 her daughter-in-law Rachel planted on the slope below the Camellia Walk a *Pinus canariensis*. Regularly the children would help pick fruit, and George in particular was not too proud to sell the produce, 'rather more than half an acre of apples and gooseberries', he wrote in 1918, and in 1924, 'busy selling peaches apples and pears to Kinsman Borne and Parnell'. Elsewhere there are references to the fruit trees which George so proudly grew in the walled garden, and also from this time there is mention in the garden of that good old standby, goldenrod, and *Nerine bowdenii*, which may have crept in from South Africa through a connection with the family of Cornish-Bowden, along with *Ornithogalum thyrsoides*, in those days known as chincherinchee, the sound produced if the stems are rubbed the one against the other. (Its genus is known colloquially as Star of Bethlehem, and if hardy enough would be a wonderful candidate for ground cover in the Holy Corner.)

In 1905 George's daughter Meg planted a maple on the bank beyond the pond, where it could be seen from the house. In April 1913, together with his other children Dorothy, Erica and Romney, she helped him with some hoeing. In the autumn of that year Dorothy, Annette and Erica helped to plant daffodils, narcissi and snowdrops; and one day in the winter George's wife had a fine bonfire in the garden. They were all obviously prepared to get their hands really dirty. In the summer of 1920, 'Miss Marsh persuaded ASF to put on an old mac over bathing dress and get into the pond and pull out big lumps of water plantain roots'. It might have been the other way round, for by that time Annette was in her thirties, and in a position to ask Miss Marsh, who was some kind of governess, or lady's companion, to jump into the pond for her, and perform this simple task. Eating cucumber sandwiches on the terrace with my great aunt Annette, half a century later, as she was beginning to look like an Italian Renaissance painting of an old lady with a high forehead, it was curious to ponder on the suitability of her behaviour years before, at a time when most people of her background would, and should have been, eating cucumber sandwiches.

The Foxes were not merely the leisured class, airily commanding plants and vistas into place. They were also clearly ahead of their time in not toeing the traditional female line. They all took an active interest and, what is more, with some sacrifice of personal comfort: there are plenty of examples of members of the family arising at 5 or 6 a.m. to ride out to Glendurgan and put in an hour's work before breakfast. Often it was moonlight when they returned home.

Nearly 100 years after Barclay had expressed in his diary his joy at moving to Penjerrick, and his reservations – 'far beyond any pecuniary advantages' – George found himself in the same predicament, and no doubt there have since been other descendants who have had similar feelings. In December 1923 George wrote:

Cuthbert, Dorothy and Annette, 1898

> Had family talk about going to Glendn - wife & self Cuth. Dor Ann Meg & Rom. I referred to its start 1821 – 1825 father's buying & planting it. His marrying & settling at Wodehouse Place and his & Mother's always living here whilst enjoying Glendn at intervals… If this house… W'ho Place can be sold fairly well it would help our getting there as Glendn is an expensive place to keep up & Income Tax & Rateable values have greatly increased & the pros & cons are considerable both ways as to moving at my age.
>
> Cuth. & Rom. were both strongly in favour of our going there at once… Rachel is quite content either way – but wishes in any case to keep herself as free as maybe for the special work & interests which she feels called to devote herself mainly to now. Meg said she would love to go there. Ann said she is not frightfully keen for the change herself but thinks it is the right thing to do. Dor said she thought she could get on there as well as anywhere with our family. All our nearest relations would like to see us there, or many of them have

said as much. It has been enjoyed & so loved by Father & Mother's descendants that it seems almost a family duty to carry on there as the family home if possible in hope of future generations being privileged & able to do the same. Its beauty in trees & landscape etc seems to increase as well as our love for it which our enjoyment of the cottage in hand at Durgan for 8 or 9 years will have enhanced.

In this way George, aged 78, became the second generation to live at Glendurgan. The news must have travelled very quickly, for on the same day his sister Lucy Hodgkin wrote a congratulatory letter:

Treworgan
Falmouth
23.12.23
Beloved George
Thou hast given me the best Christmas gift I could have now
– with this glad hope of your living at the dearly loved Glendurgan
the home of so much romance of the happiest memories
To have you within possible daily reach will mean more than I can
ever express – and I have such a strong sense that it is all in the
Divine Guidance that Glendurgan should be blessed once again
with thy management & oversight… so I am singing songs of
thanksgiving all today…
Thine fondly
Lucy

Dorothy, Cuthbert, Meg,
George, Rachel,
Erica, Romney and Annette,
Wodehouse Place, 1909

George Fox and five of his 11 siblings

George, Rachel, Dorothy, Erica, Romney, Annette, Meg, Cuthbert, Wodehouse Place, 1909

George and Rachel with members of the family and household

GARDEN DUTY
THE THIRD AND FOURTH GENERATIONS
CHAPTER SIX

This is a word to thank you for your kindness in showing me Glendurgan last week. An inadequate one, I fear – for how can one adequately express a place like that in the perfection of its beauty? Horace Walpole tried to with Strawberry Hill again and again in his letters – and sometimes he succeeds in giving just that feeling you must have when you come round the corner of your drive, after being away, and <u>catch</u> the place looking like that. Of course, I couldn't in a way quite take it in the day I was there – not consciously. It <u>was</u> too much. But I don't think my unconscious – all that goes on underneath the level of rational discourse – let me down. I found all that evening and next day when I came back there was the picture indelibly in my mind – just round the corner of one's eye, in the way some of the most valuable experiences of life are.'

(Letter from A.L. Rowse to Cuthbert and Moyra Fox, spring 1945)

The garden in the 1940s

The mid 1930s were a difficult time for my grandfather Cuthbert to take over the property. The growth of trees, although often impeded by war, has no regard for it, and during those years the garden began to see the fruit of all Alfred's endeavours, and George's too. In the absence of massive tree canopy and general tree management (very few trees were planted during the wars), plants had grown sideways into huge clumps, and the garden had a mature and luxuriant appearance. It had not been touched by tourism or the policies of serious tree management, environmental awareness, Health and Safety, or, dare one say it, gardening mania. Gardens such as Glendurgan were still private, and entering it for the first time was like coming across some kind of secret world, as anyone who ventured to steal apples and pears, or conkers, might testify. Metaphorically, but as used to be the case, one slipped under a fence, walked through a field of wheat, found a Stonehenge, and except for aesthetes like Dr Rowse, more often than not said nothing about it. Trenarren, a property he later rented in Cornwall, was, in many ways, like a mini-version of Glendurgan.

Another 'thank you' letter, treasured by my grandmother not for its eloquence but for its accuracy – and even that is questionable – came from France. It reads flatteringly:

> We cannot say how grateful we are not only for the marvellous sight you gave us of all this beauty you have created, but also for your presence: it is inappreciable to be introduced to his painting by the painter himself.

This remark might have been aimed more deservedly at Gertrude Jekyll for one of her herbaceous creations.

My grandmother was one of the first women to be married into the Fox family outside the Quaker sect. She brought with her a short-lived, but nonetheless glorious, contribution to the garden's history – that of an indulgently decorative herbaceous border. She even had a stab at a white garden. Her arrival within the Fox family coincided with an age which, since the second half of the nineteenth century, had started to witness the liberation of Quakers: they were being admitted to university and mixing more with the higher echelons of society. For some this was a social accident, but for others it became a conscious step up the social ladder, and this is recognized in gardens as much as elsewhere.

Although peonies must have permeated the borders of some of the 'gay', as opposed to 'grey' or plain Quaker fraternity – in other words the borders of the more prosperous and more liberated English cousins – it is likely that in the more Puritan families such flamboyant flowers were rather new. A parallel could perhaps be drawn with the drawing-room at Wodehouse Place, Alfred's town house, where Elton Fox recalls that the only ornaments, apart from the ubiquitous miniatures, were 'natural "specimens" – a lump of rock crystal,

The walled garden in the 1960s

a case of humming birds, ostrich eggs, and iridescent, peacock hued tropical shells'.

Now that we live in an age where money is being thrown at and into gardens it is amusing to think of those Fox ladies who worked hard in the flowerbeds. Whether to encourage or reward, my grandfather gave my grandmother a nurse's watch to be pinned to her dress. But, she said, it was to save her wristwatch from slipping off into the soil, her hand forever being among the weeds;

and the weeds, others said, forever being left in little piles, the unofficial purpose of which was to prompt collection by the gardeners.

Sprawling decoratively across the paths of the walled garden were gladioluses, very much a head gardener's plant for local summer flower shows. But my grandmother brought with her a heritage of properly bedded-out walled gardens full of cutting flowers: *Dahlia* 'Coltness Gem' presumably came from her mother's own home of that name in Lanarkshire. The garden moved into a decorative phase with the introduction of, among and amongst other things, old roses, peonies, phlox, irises, achilleas, *Limonium platyphyllum* (syn. *L. latifolium*), *Ceratostigma plumbaginoides*, delphiniums and zinnias, Michaelmas daisies, spring and autumn flowering bulbs, and pink lilies-of-the-valley. Rewarding too for a Cornish garden, was the experience to be gained from the introduction of perennials and annuals, a matter of course for the more serious estates such as Heligan, but hitherto, and even today, largely untapped in many Cornish woodland gardens. Life did exist beyond rhododendrons, camellias, magnolias and hydrangeas. But due partly to climate, and partly to the demands of the rest of the garden, and old age, this short-lived chapter gradually came to an end. So too, incidentally, did some rather nice plant names: Funkias were suddenly to be called Hostas, and Benthamias became Cornuses. The post-war efforts at Glendurgan to create an herbaceous and decorative border did not prosper in quite the same way as could be appreciated in other English gardens. Additionally, as was to become clear, in any garden open to the critical eye of the public, herbaceous borders are often the only measure of success, and therefore have to be perfect, which with one or two exceptions, is a difficult and expensive task in Cornwall. Apart from anything else, the family was reluctant to include some of the public's favourites for the successful border – one example at that time being begonias.

By the late 1950s and early 1960s my grandfather Cuthbert had already witnessed the handing over of other famous Cornish gardens to the National Trust, and he began to foresee the inherent difficulties of not only preserving, but maintaining, a garden like Glendurgan. This is separate from any anxieties he might have had over taxation. Unlike some estates, there were no agricultural yields, or rental income to fund the garden. In any event, cross-subsidising can be a questionable policy, as was the suggestion at one point that the garden could be run from any proceeds made out of the family's business activities.

At the time, the idea of giving away an inheritance must have been unpalatable, especially for my father who represented the next generation. However, in the light of what has happened since the 1960s, and of what was not foreseen, it was a correct but nonetheless hard decision. The demonstration is to be seen not only in the progress of the garden, but also in the lack of progress in those gardens that are now experiencing problems of preservation and maintenance. It is noticeable that those that succeed, or have some chance of succeeding, are those where some kind of radical action has been taken. Usually this involves the adrenalin of the younger generation, such as Tim Smit, who has been responsible for the success of Heligan. But that is not always the case: Major Hibbert had intended that Trebah would be his retirement home, and not the premier garden that, by his sterling efforts, it has now become. It is also apparent that in order for all these beautiful places to survive, duty has to be paid to them rather than to their owners. It does not necessarily follow that this course of action is going to coincide with the emotions of their owners. Glendurgan is an exception.

Nor can the emotions of an owner easily control the future destiny of his or her inheritance. A trust can be set up, but unless it really merits it, and is established professionally, there is a danger that the pioneering spirit behind the trust will eventually evaporate. Presumably this is one very good reason why the National Trust is keen to continue with a reasonable involvement of its donor families. The disintegration of private trusts is particularly tragic if the nature of the property is such that it could easily have been bought by a private person with sufficient funds for its improvement and maintenance. This obviates the need for a trust, and leaves one person in control, with both responsibility and authority under one hat. Curiously, we seem to have entered an economic era where this is now happening. However, it had not happened in 1962, when my grandparents and my father donated Glendurgan, with an endowment, to the National Trust.

The garden is now in safe hands and, as it turns out, the change in ownership is blessed by the fact that Glendurgan can continue to be enjoyed by my family. In the list of contributions made by successive generations towards the history of the garden, recognition and credit must go to the donor generations for the decision they took. It represented not only years of heartache, but a thorough investigation into all the alternatives, and then the lengthy process of negotiation with the National Trust. The evidence of this was in a deluge of papers which flooded my grandparents' desks for months and months; and it must have required a good deal of dutiful perseverance to have brought the gift to its fruition. The gift rendered incalculable benefits not to the family so much as to the garden. What else would have happened? Pleasing decay and dereliction? Incompetent and unrealistic family-run trusts? The decimation and bedecking of walled gardens into desirable residences of a single-storey nature, this characteristic being seen by the planners as a concession to the listing of tall and once fruitful walls? The sale of a beautiful property to some monied individual who has little good taste, let alone horticultural knowledge? All these possibilities are undesirable, especially in respect of what the National Trust has been able to achieve.

In the early 1960s the National Trust's Garden Adviser, Graham Stuart Thomas, must have been introduced to the family by the Trust, in particular as a leading authority on roses. He and my grandparents were often to be seen in deep consultation on the pros and cons of various roses, until then a relatively unexplored genus at Glendurgan, and in general a plant that is not seen at its best in Cornwall. The upshot of this was the emergence in the walled garden of a line of *Rosa* 'Queen Elizabeth', highly suitable for cutting, and three big round beds featuring *Rosa* 'Allgold', *Rosa* 'Iceberg', and *Rosa* 'Orange Sensation'. They looked incredibly smart. There were, of course, other, older roses in the walled garden, but the new circular beds were very much the style of gardening in the 1960s. To give another example, demonstrating the advances made in garden education, my grandmother, who was a knowledgeable amateur gardener, made the following note in 1975 about a plant which has now become popular: 'ground cover 'Lamium' little pale yellow bell attractive leaf – in wall garden from Hidcote', a note which neither she nor the gardeners at Hidcote would be proud of today. Design was not a criterion, but catalogues were; and I have memories of my grandmother spending hours at her desk ordering bulbs. Those got walloped into the ground in order to provide colour before the roses, suggested by Graham Thomas, came into bloom.

From the early history of the National Trust at Glendurgan, under the management of my father, Philip, what will never be seen again are the scores of letters personally dictated and signed by individuals who were then at management level, but who have now risen to, and retired from, positions of eminence within the Trust. Letters, now over taken by email messages, were exchanged daily on a whole range of subjects, and usually at a rate of one subject per letter, such as replacing an Atco lawnmower for a few pounds shillings and pence, ordering plants, reporting an accident, obtaining quotes for gravel, opening times, collecting rents, personnel matters, the rights of hedgehogs, etc. It was a difficult time: difficult for my father, who understandably was aggrieved at being the first generation not to have had a time in the chair, and who was now having to adopt a profession for which he had received no formal training in land management or anything else, and under the authority of a new owner. It was difficult for the National Trust. On the one hand it bent

A National Trust meeting

over backwards in trying to be sensitive towards the family, and to decipher its likes and dislikes, while on the other hand, as the new owner, it sought to implement changes. Every member of the family was allowed to attend the meetings on site, with an overwhelming representation from the Trust's office and gardening staff – once I counted a total of 14 – which meant that individuals wandered off into little disparate groups. One of these groups might then spend half an hour delving into the pages of at least six heavy garden-design books in order to select a new garden seat. Another group would be engaged in an argument over the family's dislike of a particular genus, which the Trust wanted to introduce – although significantly it was quite happy to be led on roses. It was even more difficult for the head gardener, who was used to having a personal relationship with the family, but who now had another boss, to whom he was occasionally keen to show some initiative, such initiative not always receiving the endorsement of the family.

Another aspect of the garden, to be remembered with relief from the time of the handover, was that in fact very little changed, rose-beds excepted. It was rather like a wood I once came across miles from anywhere, with a label on its entrance gate stating: 'This wood is the property of such and such a charity…'. No hype. Contributions to the upkeep of the garden were voluntary, and my mother emptied the contents of the money boxes into old canvas bags. This was done on behalf of my father who was the manager. Occasionally she met the odd visitor in the garden. Although it was open for only a few days each week during March, April and May, the nurture of both winter-flowering and summer-flowering plants continued to receive equal attention. It is true that some plants were recognized as special, but the awareness of Glendurgan as a horticultural garden of note had not then begun in earnest. Neither had it fully dawned on us that trees and shrubs are a crop, and that therefore the garden, in spite of being entrusted, was inevitably going to change.

HORTICULTURE
CHAPTER SEVEN

'A learned man
Could give it a clumsy name.
Let him name it who can,
The beauty would be the same.'

(*Alfred, Lord Tennyson*, Maud: A Monodrama, *Part II, ii, 1855*)

The fame of the more recent gardens in Cornwall has sometimes made it easy to forget that gardening history was running its course in Cornwall as much as in any other part of the country. At Boconnoc, the sixteenth-century deer park still survives. The seventeenth century saw the usual influences of Italy and the Grand Tour here as elsewhere, and in the eighteenth century, even though 'Capability' Brown never came to Cornwall, his followers built their houses 'grazing' in their own landscapes. At the end of the century Humphry Repton visited the important gardens of Antony, Port Eliot, and Tregothnan, preparing his 'Red Books' for them, as well as for Catchfrench which, as ear-

lier observed, was the first house occupied by the Fox family in Cornwall. The Victorian passion for greenhouses and conservatories, rockeries and carpet bedding provoked a reaction from William Robinson, who became an advocate for the 'natural garden'. These changes in fashion were subconsciously adapted by the Cornish to their own use.

Of far more importance in Cornwall during the nineteenth century, however, was the influence of the plant hunters. Robert Were Fox at Penjerrick was among the first to receive seed from the Himalayan rhododendrons collected during the expeditions of Sir Joseph Hooker. His daughter Anna Maria, who was acquainted with Hooker, appointed Samuel Smith as her gardener. He became a skilled

Anna Maria Fox

hybridizer of these rhododendrons, and it cannot be for nothing that Hamilton Davey wrote, 'how much Cornwall owes to Penjerrick is a question she may never learn to answer quite justly'.

Other families, such as the Williamses, and especially J.C. Williams of Caerhays Castle – which of all the Cornish gardens most closely resembles a Himalayan hillside – financed expeditions; and they were joined later by Col. Bolitho of Trengwainton, now a National Trust garden, and George Johnstone of Trewithen. The Foxes at Penjerrick had some contact with Kew, but nothing like

Tregrehan

Myosotidium hortensia

that of the Dorrien-Smiths on Tresco. J.D. Enys of Enys sent home many plants and seeds from New Zealand, including the remarkable Chatham Island forget-me-not, *Myosotidium hortensia*. The blue of these blooms is of a Mediterranean hue so intense that they were later grown at a famous Cornish garden in order to grace the visits of the Queen Mother in the 1960s. The royal household's suppliers could also show tact, by obtaining *Lachenalia aloides* from another Cornish garden to match the national colours of Jordan for a state visit of King Hussein.

Veitch, the Exeter nursery, had sent Thomas Lobb to Java, and his brother William to North and South America, whence he returned with, among many other introductions, *Embothrium coccineum*. This was extensively planted in the beautiful garden at Carclew, where their father was employed by Sir Charles Lemon. Nigel Holman of Chyverton tells a story of an enthusiastic visitor who once approached a later incumbent at Carclew, saying, 'Madam I understand that you have the finest collection of embothriums in all Cornwall.' Being very deaf, and thinking he had said 'bathrooms', she replied, 'Well, actually we have four; did you wish to use one now?'

Embothrium coccineum

Sir Charles Lemon, who had no son, was followed at Carclew by his son-in-law John Tremayne of Heligan, an example of the many cross-connections which were strong at that time between the owners of the great estates; they also shared their gardeners and used the same architects. Many Victorian land-owners were ruled by ambition and investment, but on balance in Cornwall it appears to have been an age of discovery and co-operation rather than imitation and competition. Certainly that was what happened between members of the Fox family and their head gardeners who exhibited so enthusiastically at the Falmouth spring flower shows. Robert Barclay, for instance, finding he must clear out some of his seedlings and other rhododendrons to make room at Penjerrick gave Lucy Hodgkin a dozen rhodos for Treworgan and GHF 23 for Glendurgan… Glory of Penjerrick crossed with *Thomsonii* and also all of the Barclayi class including one called Robert Fox (*Rhododendron* 'Barclayi' Robert Fox).

Penjerrick, notwithstanding its additional generosity to many other Cornish gardens, remains abundant with rhododendrons.

The Foxes became accomplished hybridizers, and are remembered in this context for their rhododendrons: 'Barclayi Helen Fox' and 'Budock' in addition to those already mentioned. J.G. Millais in his classic book *Rhododendrons* wrote:

Rhododendron 'Penjerrick'

three exceptional Rhododendrons… claim Trebah as their first home… these being R. 'Trebianum', R. 'Trebah Gem' [photographs pages 50–51] and R. 'Edmondii', a hybrid between *R. arboreum* and *R. barbatum* which originated in the garden, the seedling having been sent to Mr Fox… from Tremough. This is without doubt one of the most brilliant and valuable hybrids that have appeared.

The second Lord Aberconway of Bodnant, a garden against which most Cornish gardens pale into insignificance, was of the opinion that *Rhododendron* 'Penjerrick', one of several achieved by Samuel Smith, was the finest rhododendron hybrid ever raised. I recall visiting with my grandmother another head gardener from Penjerrick, Bert Evans. She was very proud to present him with a trug containing one or two sprigs from Glendurgan, until Mrs Evans suggested that her husband should show us what he had at the back of their bungalow. He escorted us to a small greenhouse dominated by what appeared to be the scent and sight of the most magnificent *Lilium regale*, but which on closer examination turned out to be a hybrid rhododendron, one of the parents being *R. crassum*, or some such sweet-smelling species. One thousand seeds had been dispatched to Lionel Fortescue at The Garden House in Devon, but despite better equipment there, had failed to germinate, whereas Bert Evans, with the minimum of facilities, had succeeded in producing a masterpiece. Typically, and disappointingly, he had no wish to take it a stage further – such was the humility of the old-fashioned type of head gardener.

One of the pleasures of living in Cornwall during the winter is being surrounded by fields of daffodils which stripe the landscape, grown for the bulb market. For about a hundred years from 1870 both large and small gardens became regular

suppliers by rail of flowers and foliage to Cov-
ent Garden Market in London. Glendurgan and
Trebah were no exception, although it may seem
inconceivable today that there could have been
any significant economic return from this trade.
Growers rose early and stayed up late, under the
dim gleam of single light-bulbs, in order to perfect posy after posy of primroses, snowdrops and
ivy, violets, anemones, cyclamens and, from the
tenanted wintry fields of Glendurgan, slender
pencil buds of *Iris unguicularis*. Trebah excelled
in Belladonna lilies. Now that market gardening
has decreased, it is not uncommon to come across
stands of outgrown pittosporum or vagrant nar-

cissi; indeed some types of bulb, such as the Scillonian Whistling Jack, *Gladiolus communis* subsp. *byzantinus*, have now become naturalized, and recently at Glendurgan some of the daffodil species once grown commercially have been encouraged to grow in woodland areas. Similarly, vestigial apple trees, especially at Glendurgan, are reminders that orchards and walled gardens were once a vital part of any estate.

The Foxes were keen and knowledgeable fruit growers. On 1 May 1844 Alfred wrote that there was at Glendurgan 'a garden with wall

eleven foot high well stocked with peach and nectarine trees, meadows, orchards etc... some one hundred sort of apples and upwards of fifty sort of pears.' Meanwhile, in the gardens of their houses on the outskirts of Falmouth, George Croker Fox was awarded the Banksian

Medal of the Royal Horticultural Society of Cornwall for acclimatizing 223 foreign plants in the open at Grove Hill. At Rosehill, the house of his cousin Robert Were Fox, a French visitor wrote:

> The orange, date and lemon trees pass the winter here in the open air, grow freely and bear ripe fruit. I saw a tree there from which one hundred and twenty three lemons were plucked in one day, all excellent and much sweeter than those sold in the shops.

Edgar Thurston, in *Trees and Shrubs in Cornwall*, published in 1930, wrote that at Glendurgan 'at one time there were as many as one hundred and thirty varieties' of pear. Apparently Alfred liked to cut up several different samples of pear and offer them around like a cheese board; and I have a vague memory of the fruit being labelled not only in the garden, but also on the sideboard in the dining room. In October 1844 Alfred recorded that 'one of my Jersey pears weighs 19 ounces', and in November of the same year he planted 60 pear trees in Birch's orchard. On 27 March 1846 he referred again to the pears: 'most of my pear blossoms not yet open except "Chaumontel", "Easter Beurre" and "Duchesse d'Angouleme".' His son George also prided himself on a superb collection of fruit trees, and in the fruit trees, mistletoe. Here are some extracts from his notebooks:

> 1913 'Cornish Aromatic' and 'Adam's Permain' kept till mid March but were shrivelling up. A very good crop of 'Newton Wonder' and good colour. Kept some till mid March or later. 'Dummellor's Seedling' from one tree were very fine and kept well middle of April or later. A hard green apple from one tree well cropped kept till middle of April or later called 'Gloria Mundi'.
> 1914 April 16: Few apples still keeping – 'Lord Derby' – 'Bramley's Seedling' 'Newton Wonder'… Kitty Ridges grafted middle of three grafted trees in bottom row – with 'Gascoyne's Scarlet' of ten grafts three or four grew.

Perhaps most remarkable was the performance of tender plants. In 1922 George wrote: 'Peaches set well and nectarines and pears and apples promising… the out of door citrus has several yellow fruit on it.' Despite the change in climate, the evidence today is that citrus trees do not survive the rigours of our Cornish winters.

Glendurgan's horticultural status depends upon the garden's micro-climate, which to a great extent is due to the shelter belts. The planting of these was one of Alfred's first tasks, in the face of windy views out towards the mouth of the River Helford. In 1826 he received from Messrs Beck, Allan & Shearman, seedsmen, a bill which included '2000 Scotch Firs for 12/-, 1000 Silver Firs for 16/-, 1000 Scotch Elm for 5/-, 1000 Norway Spruce for 3/6, 1000 Larch for 4/-, 1000 Oak for 12/-'.

In 1832 he was 'busy planting silver and spruce firs', and in 1846 he put in 76 *Pinus nigra* and pinasters along the Schoolroom Walk. George carried on this tradition, as is seen from the following extracts:

> February 1 1926 – ASF having ordered one hundred two foot Scotch Firs as a present from her to Glendurgan from Veitch of Exeter at ten shillings per one hundred (Treseders Truro quoted nine shillings per dozen, one and a half foot high). She, W.E. and I chose place where they may be planted. Inside front gate on east side of drive, below Camellia Walk adjoining the hedge where a Turkey Oak and Silver Fir were blown over into the field by a South West gale last winter, top north east end of old kitchen garden, open space on East Hill where two Silvers were thrown down by South West gales last winter, further end of Manderson's Hill which used to be orchard, a field near the old Schoolroom, and a field behind the wall garden for stock.

He also had the extra task of thinning and felling where some of Alfred's trees were beginning to block the view:

> November 28 1924 – Norman Sothern, Annette, Meg and GHF decided to ascertain whether it was a Douglas Fir on Manderson's Hill whose top was running up fast to hide the view of the Helford River from this dining room window or another evergreen tree as Annette thought and while Meg stayed at the house Norman climbed the Douglas Fir with a white cloth and thought it was not the tree GHF thought and Norman then climbed another *Thuja lobbii [plicata]* which proved to be the one that will have to be cut down. We then went to a Turkey oak at the edge of the cliff in H. Y. Pascoe's (tenant) orchard and with a bamboo and white cloth he climbed it and fixed the bamboo at the top and on returning to the house we saw the white flag and it proved to be the tree which is hiding part of the river. GHF was told HP (or his sons-in-law) might cut it down and though he is not well enough to do it himself he felt sure his sons-in-law would do it for the wood of the tree.

Two years later George was at it again, this time losing three ornamental healthy trees which, he said, went to his 'heart as well as theirs to cut down'.

In the interests of preserving and improving the garden's micro-climate, the National Trust has, by planting up fields of mixed forest trees either side of and behind the garden, improved on the original idea of shelter belts, and braces, one might even say. Judicious thinning also continues. The gardeners are trained in tree-felling, and questions of arboriculture are treated seriously. At a garden meeting there was once a problem in identifying from the head of the valley a beech that had begun to obscure the view. The triangular peep of the river, and the romantically beckoning stretch of sand at Bosahan on the opposite shore, were beginning to disappear. 'Now where is that beech?' asked John Sales, the Trust's gardens adviser, peering down at the view from the house. 'Bosahan' came the unintentionally witty reply. It happened to be 1 April, and we had already fooled the garden's adviser into marvelling, momentarily, at the progress of spring with bunches of bananas attached to the plant, and from behind some bushes my father enthusiastically, and only slightly less than accurately, imitating a cuckoo.

The cultivation of tender and hardy exotic plants has become a central theme of the garden, but in a way that was originally experimental, and certainly amateur. This does not deny the fact that the plant lists of over 100 years ago were impressive, and often extravagant: it must have been amazing to behold all that the Victorian plant hunters were introducing. It is just odd that, despite the extensive knowledge of the various Foxes who have lived and gardened in Cornwall, it is only with the passage of years that their gardens have become horticulturally outstanding. A letter written in 1957 from Vita Sackville-West to my grandmother about a rosemary is also that of an amateur, whatever history might have to say about the respective gardens of Sissinghurst or Glendurgan; and it is very revealing to compare mid-twentieth century photographs of both gardens. Having achieved horticultural status, Glendurgan is now managed along very professional lines, and this in itself reflects a significant development. Compare an entry from George's diary in 1914, highlighting the family's penchant for commemorative plants, with an extract from a garden report issued at the turn of the twentieth century:

> Dec 2 To commemorate year of the war and Cuthbert being a commissioned officer in R. E. Territorial Cornwall stationed at Penryn we planted around or near this orchard R. J. F. a larch, G. H. F. Tulip tree, Cuthbert 4 Scotch (sic) Firs, Annette a Cedrus deodara and purple Beech, Erica Willow leaf oak *Quercus louetta* [*Quercus phellos*], Meg Birch and common Beech.

> Plant more *Bupleurum fruticosum* and *Drimys winteri* mixed to screen path. Further on interplant scented rhododendrons with own *Rh. decorum*. Add to group of *Hydrangea* 'Ayesha', remove sickly rhododendron, plant 50 *Gladiolus byzantinus*; at back remove more laurel and plant 5 *Hoheria* 'Stardust'. Pollard Ilex

Devolving from this horticultural professionalism, the National Trust has shown sensitivity to the maturity of a Victorian garden and, despite the family's contributions described above, to a lack of planting during the two world wars. The result has been a generous replacement of many old trees. This, together with current Health and Safety requirements, are justifiable defences to frequent, uninformed criticism, which refers to the garden being over tidy and – a new verb – 'National Trustified'. Putting this positively, as a friend so encouragingly remarked, 'The *weedlessness* at Glendurgan is astonishing'. The National Trust takes its entrusted responsibilities seriously, and it is articulate on numerous gardening subjects, not least of which is the introduction of rare species. I was impressed recently to see the list of magnolias alone grown at Glendurgan. The Trust also advises with authority on matters of maintenance and, what is more, knows how to implement its advice. An instance of this was the felling of a giant *Pinus radiata*, which was so large it had 12 small trees and shrubs growing out of it, and was beginning to obscure the view of the river. Clara Vyvyan from Trelowarren had once commented that we needed to apply our shears to it, and she returned the following year to observe sarcastically that we had had a go with our nail scissors. If the tree had been left to its own devices it is likely that it would have come down, causing severe damage to everything in its path. Storm damage did occur in 1990, when a *Cedrus atlantica* Glauca Group collapsed on to a *Cedrus deodara* growing on the island in the pond. With usual application to purpose, and within a month of opening to the public, the National Trust had organized the removal of this tree with the debris of about 40 other trees, many of which had fallen awkwardly. On the whole, however, God has been kind, most notably in 1998 when a *Thuja plicata*, known affectionately as the Pirate's Tree because of its far-fetched likeness to a ship, came down in a high wind, no more than clipping the

Pinus radiata

Michelia doltsopa below it. To save the gravel paths, and because of the size of the trunks on a steep slope, the gardeners created a track whereby the tree could be dragged up the hill and out of the main body of the garden.

Since the National Trust's ownership, there have been many examples of how the practice of effective gardening can be ruthless. One of the best of these is the restoration of the maze. Having always had an embarrassingly superficial knowledge of the maze, I decided in 1968 to make a drawing of its plan. On comparing this with the original, which must have been used for planting

Glendurgan maze
showing original
plan, restoration
in progress, and
on completion

in 1833, it was easy to spot several defects in the design. In addition to all the holes where visitors had pushed their way through, or out of, the maze, the general condition was very poor. 1991 was known nationally as the Year of the Maze, which seemed a suitable time to launch a major reconstruction. It succeeded largely due to the enthusiasm of the head gardener at that time, Robert James, and to the support of the National Trust's garden adviser, John Sales. The maze was restored to its original pattern based on one, now no longer in existence, at the Sydney Gardens in Bath. Huge wadges of irrelevant laurel and hydrangea were removed, weeds and sapling trees eradicated, paths drained and rebuilt, and the original laurel hedges reduced to ground level. At this stage the maze was a bare brown patch with new shoots of laurel breaking through like trails of bright green paint. Finally, the maze was crowned by a summerhouse modelled on one that had stood there a hundred years ago, with on its floor a symbolic pebble mosaic of three fishes.

Would these drastic measures have been taken had the garden remained within private ownership? I doubt it. National Trust ownership results in a standard that exceeds the original standard of the donated garden. It is inevitable, and because it represents progress is not necessarily a bad thing. Hence Glendurgan is now squarely in the running as a unique repository for exotic plants, and a centre for the purposeful propagation of rare and tender species. Not everyone is aware of this. To put things into perspective, *Cunninghamia konishii* is less common than the giant panda, but not, in my experience, as easy to recognize. Christopher Page, a friend who was for 25 years the Principal Scientific Officer of the Royal Botanic Garden, Edinburgh, is responsible for the introduction of other conifers of a tender nature; and the last garden adviser to the National Trust, John Sales, is responsible for an embryonic Bhutanese valley in the lower part of the garden – an idea which receives my support following a trip I also made to the rhododendron groves and conifer-clad hills of the Himalayas.

In examining Glendurgan's horticultural status, one final point has to be emphasized, which has only come to light since the garden has begun to receive large numbers of visitors from all parts of the world. Some of these are dendrologists; some are serious gardeners; some are professional, and many are amateur. They all look for excellence, whether or not what they see is familiar. With the surge of interest in gardening matters, particularly through the educative media of television and magazines, it is vital that the garden never flags or grows stale. The only measure of judgement any visitor has is his or her own very valid experience, and in that way the garden has to appeal to all tastes.

Recently, conscious efforts have been made in the way of plant labelling – an almost impossible task. Leaving aside any aesthetic considerations, where does labelling start, and where does it end? Once a Swedish captain came to Glendurgan and was asked to name his favourite plant. '*Ulex europaeus*,' came the reply, to which my grandmother said how much she admired the blue variety – she knew her plants, but as is human nature gave her acquaintances, and herself, the impression that she knew rather more than the truth would allow. On the way back to his ship it was learnt that the common name for this plant is gorse, still unavailable in blue, as far as I know.

For the unenlightened, should a handsome but common plant, such as *Agapanthus* be labelled? If, however, such a common plant has another more colloquial and well-known name, for example 'arum lily', is the public to be denied the opportunity of learning that properly this plant rejoices under the distinguished name of *Zantedeschia aethiopica*? Curiously, the words *Gunnera manicata*, loved and used with abandon by garden designers, now run off everyone's tongue much more easily than giant rhubarb. This plant can most effectively be placed in the moats of large castles, to be admired from a height of 50 feet or more. For the amateur gardener, does everything have to be labelled, often at the risk of the gardening staff being told that a plant has been either omitted or incorrectly labelled? A label I observed on one occasion, and never again, in a nearby garden was attached to a rhododendron but read *Convolvulus mauritanicus*, tempting smiles or criticism from some, creating confusion for others. As for the professionals who can tell plants by leaf and bark as much as by flower, do they need to be told about *Camellia* 'Donation'? This raises another question for them: does the garden gain from this particular camellia? The beginner, however, is looking for the lowest common denominator, and its label. There is that psychological quirk we all have, at whatever

level of knowledge, for verbalizing our identifications. It is almost as if the object being identified has to be captured, the competition won, and our security boosted. The irony is that actually the common denominator of the gardening world is the use of Latin names, which, subject to the whims of taxonomists, are accessible to anyone anywhere in the world. It is the cause and effect of gardening mania that the horticultural boundaries are pushed, which properly results in the reputation the Trust has for providing, albeit often unwittingly, sound gardening education, and not only for adults.

Zantedeschia aethiopica

THE GARDEN
CHAPTER EIGHT

*'The Handkerchief or Ghost Tree
stands among Monterey pines
The Californian redwood, the Chilean
Fire Bush, the Whitebeam, the Maidenhair
Tree, in the Garden of Glendurgan
That slopes to the Helford River,
to the quiet beach of Durgan…
this convocation of
the world's trees, massing now
into one, without losing their distinct
character, in the walk down to Durgan.'*

(D.M. Thomas)

As fashions change, and as plants die and are replaced, any garden guide will become out of date. What I hope will never become out of date, however, is the inclusion of the plants mentioned in the following paragraphs, for they are some of the plants which give Glendurgan its unchanging character.

Cornish gardens are well known for their colour in the spring, and Glendurgan is known as a spring garden. Efforts have been made, particularly since the National Trust's ownership, to continue this season of colour into the summer and autumn. As a result, summer breaks in a wave of whiteness with *Eucryphia*, *Hoheria*, *Myrtus*, and that 'bombe Alaska' of rhododendrons 'Polar Bear', while autumn is awash with bulbs such as *Amaryllis*, *Colchicum*, *Crinum*, and *Nerine*. But what seems to be overlooked is that Glendurgan grows a great variety of trees notable at any time of the year.

The most famous of these are the tulip trees, some of the oldest and largest in northern Europe. If there were theme tunes for trees, *Liriodendron tulipifera* would have 'The Star-Spangled Banner'. Elephantine in size and skin, these Americans are stylish, brave, generous, jazzy and relentless. I love their sheer zest for life: even the leaf buds in spring open like the arms of a ground controller conducting the movements of aircraft. For a time the leaves remain

Eucryphia x nymansensis 'Nymansay'

Leaf buds of Liriodendron tulipifera

like flags at 10 o'clock and 2 o'clock; then they open from being a cut-out half leaf into a strange whole leaf with one lobe apparently missing. Finally comes the flower, striped in pale orange and green. For those who want to go over the top there is even a variegated version. However, with the odd exception such as *Miscanthus sinensis* 'zebrinus', I tend to agree with my wife whose attitude to variegation is, 'Why go for the fancy version if the plain one is good enough?' The so-called tulip tree is the only genus of Liriodendroideae, a Magnoliaceae subfamily.

Liriodendron tulipifera

Ginkgo biloba

The longevity of magnolias, and sometimes the size of their blooms, designate them mammoths in the world of plants. Seemingly they take precedence over any *Prunus* in the cherry orchard, and are certainly as ancient as any apple in the Garden of Eden. Originating in the Tertiary period, the noble magnolia represents some of the earliest arrivals of plant life on this planet. Indeed, pollination is still carried out by flower beetles, rather than bees or butterflies, which millions of years ago had not evolved. *Magnolia pterocarpa* is regarded by some as being almost as old as the *Ginkgo*, and fossil

Magnolia campbellii subsp. mollicomata

remains of magnolias are common in the Tertiary strata of the Northern hemisphere. In the autumn, gardeners and non-gardeners alike cannot fail to notice the fossil-like prints of the large skeletal leaves, and wonder at their origin. In early, silent springs, from what dark twigs, from what dull bark, from what naked nothingness come the shapely displays of candles, hats, goblets and pocket handkerchiefs, all of which describe the flowers of *Magnolia denudata* and *Magnolia campbellii* ? Their fragrance and colours, white and pink to puce, represent the purity and candour symbolized by the magnolia in the illustrations of the T'ang Dynasty (AD 618–907).

Magnoliaceae are a unique family, and cannot easily be confused, unlike, for example, members of the Rosaceae and Cistaceae families. Once, however, I overheard a puzzled, and puzzling, remark made by a builder trying to reach a window through the leaves of a *Magnolia grandiflora* – 'Now petunia, tulip, or magnolia; which is it?' Enlightenment failed me, in exactly the same way as it did when an American woman on a garden tour asked her friend whether a *Verbena* was a *Viburnum*. The friend, however, was kind enough to reply authoritatively by making that sound which is spelt 'yp', and which has come to be recognized as an affirmative. So that was clearly that, but I live with the memory of allowing a builder and two women to be misled and, worse, to the detriment of any reputation I might have, with the risk of one day being corrected. (I also stand to be considered rather more generous than is the truth: one particular friend is of the misconception that I gave him a nice little maple by the unknown name of *Acer rinthe*, rather than a *Cerinthe*.)

The magnolia was given its name by a Swede, Carl Linnaeus, to honour Pierre Magnol, who lived from 1638 to 1715, and who was professor of medicine and director of Montpellier's botanic garden in the south of France. A few years ago some members of the Swedish Magnolia Society visited Glendurgan. They liked to meet on occasion to compare the number of blooms on various Swedish magnolias, but at Glendurgan they were astounded to see several towering clouds of colour: thousands of flowers on single plants. In the same way, my perspective of *Pittosporum tobira* was changed on seeing these shrubs the size of apple trees, shading the piazza of a Mediterranean village. In the light of their ordinariness they even had their trunks painted white. In California they edge public car-parks.

Pittosporum tobira edging a California car-park

Although not even recognized today as the touchstone of many a site, it is hard to imagine an English garden of any note before the introduction of *Magnolia grandiflora*. Neither is it easy to imagine a Cornish estate before the glory of the Victorian plant hunters, whose magnolia trophies have come into their own only since the turn of the nineteenth century. Yet what other plant arriving in 1877, with its inherently criss-cross pruner's nightmare, replicates so precisely the intricacies of a typical Victorian design, as *Magnolia stellata*? Its flower seems emblematic of the Victorian garden party scene, and what hat-fashions have been in pursuit of, both delicate shades of colour, and shade from the sun.

On days when it is hot and grasshoppers sing, and the only birds to be heard are buzzards and doves, there are moments when the only other sound is the breeze in the leathery leaves of *Magnolia grandiflora* or *M. delavayi*. On such days, when the garden has been bleached

Magnolia stellata

to a dull monotone, and the banks of long grass are cut, and parched, and the hydrangeas are wilting, just then the sole show of bright green will be the leaves of *Magnolia* x *thompsoniana*. The flowers are often semi-recessed beneath their greenness, but irresistibly, the lemony scent will betray their presence, hiding and retiring there like precious pieces of parchment. The intricate centres of any flower cup are worthy of an interior designer, as is the ecclesiastical colouring of seeds and flowers; and the texture of the bud-covering perules on some of the spring-flowering species is as furry as mice. The perules drop as the tepals open. The word 'tepal' was first used by the magnolia authority and author, George Johnstone, who recognized that in most magnolias there is no difference between petals and sepals. This is easy to see in his garden, Trewithen, eminent for its rich collection of Asiatic magnolias. Magnolias are an experience aesthetically and botanically, and like many plants they also have other uses. *M. denudata*, *M. virginiana*, and *M. grandiflora* are used medicinally, and *M. hypoleuca* and *M. kobus* are valued for veneering. This digression into magnolias shows how, on close examination, any plant becomes fascinat-

Magnolia x thompsoniana

ing, revealing and rewarding. If that experience is then
applied to flora in general,
therein lies the education
of a lifetime, let alone in the
words of that giant of garden designers, Russell Page,
'of a gardener'.

I must include a brief
note on copper beeches, the punctuation mark of so many English landscapes.
On very sunny days, when colour seems to have evaporated, they are the trees
that always give a depth and a sense of dimension. They also act as an excellent backdrop to pale-coloured rhododendrons, and are good too with purples
and deep blues. Shades of maroon, with the breath of light behind them, are
useful colours in a garden.

The Camellia Walk, like those at Penjerrick and Trebah, was designed to be
close to the house and on relatively flat land, for the convenient and safe per-
ambulation of long-skirted ladies. In 1924 George refers to it as 'the straight
walk'. The Williams family at Tredrea, which had previously been a Fox
home, affectionately named a similar path 'Ma's Walk', which coped satisfac-
torily with any problem of a postprandial promenade involving a hill. When

the property was subsequently sold and divided into residential plots, it somehow became renamed 'Marswaulk', much to the amusement of remaining members of the family. Like long galleries, these walks tended to be culs-de-sac, but the camellia walk at Glendurgan was made more purposeful by linking it to a new path intended to emulate the layout of the original entrance and drive to the property. *Camellia japonica* 'Preston Rose'; *Camellia japonica* 'Gloire de Nantes', and *Camellia reticulata* edge this path.

Glendurgan

Penjerrick, 1879

Once I gave a friend a pot of *Camellia sasanqua*, whose flowers on a winter's day smell sweetly of *Nicotiana*, the tobacco plant. Ten years later it was a pleasure to receive a card saying what joy this plant gave her in its maturity. In the same bracket as *Camellia sasanqua* there are other

Tredrea

Camellia sasanqua

almost non-scents, which contribute towards what wine experts might call the garden's fine nose. I could easily dispense with both the ubiquitous sedge grass and *Leycesteria*, but most gardens have to enter the world with their quota of *Iris foetidissima*, the crushed leaves of which smell, happily for the wine expert, of roast beef. Wild garlic – as a companion plant, garden designers might say – is everywhere, widely available. Winter heliotrope, which smells of an almost edible type of glue paste, is also in this group. *Pittosporum tobira* is justifiably famous for its scent of orange blossom, but often overlooked are the tiny black flowers of *Pittosporum tenuifolium*, which at night can perfume the air with honey. Now almost indigenous, one sniff of the South American *Escallonia* leaf will remind anyone of childhood holidays by the sea. The never-failing evergreen *Choisya ternata* deserves a mention, both for its aromatic leaves and its heavy scent. *Michelia doltsopa*, a beautiful evergreen, but spring-flowering member of the magnolia family has a strange, clinical smell. Most delicious is the smell of ripe wild strawberries in July. *Rhododendron luteum* is as sweet as honey. Redolent of the Mediterranean in intense heat is the cedar

Michelia doltsopa

Drimys winteri

trees' scent of incense; so are cistus leaves after rain. Elusive and subliminal upon the senses, but wonderfully delicate, are *Drimys*, *Azara*, and *Eucryphia* and, *en masse*, primula (*Primula prolifera* and *P. florindae*), bluebells, lime-tree flowers and, perhaps above all, primroses, 'Botticelli-ing,' as someone once eulogized, down the valley. With so many of these come the humming bees, the sound of the air in high summer.

One year the colours of spring were so brilliant I asked the painter Patrick Heron if he would like to come over for the day. He would surely appreciate the Sissinghurst blue of *Rhododendron augustinii*, the lime-green of *Taxodium distichum* var. *imbricatum* 'Nutans', the orange of *Embothrium*, and the Kurume

Rhododendron 'White Wings'

The dell

Hedychium gardnerianum

Beschorneria yuccoides

azaleas for good measure. Addition-ally there is in the garden a *Rhododen-dron ponticum* 'Cheiranthifolium', given to the family by William Arnold-For-ster, who had been a former owner of Patrick's house at Zennor, and who had visited Glendurgan for a week in May 1936, 'knowing names, manners of growth & habitats of nearly all plants & rhododendrons'. It is probable that at that time he introduced some origi-nal stock from Italy of *Rosmarinus* 'Tus-can Blue'. It was typical of Patrick's modesty and sensitivity that he stood still in the cherry orchard ablaze with his favourite palette, closed his eyes and said, 'But it's not just the colours; it's the profusion of scents which is so overwhelming'.

As with the camellia, no perfunc-tory 'thank you' letter followed this experience, but six months later and refreshingly, a card arrived with the message, 'I have been thinking about that day we had in the spring'.

Then there are all those ericaceous aristocrats, such as *Rhododendron* 'Countess of Haddington', *R.* 'Lady Alice Fitzwilliam', together with *R.* 'Princess Alice'. Less distinguished to the ear, but not to the nose, are *R.* 'Fragrantissimum', and *R.* 'White Wings'. The ginger plant by the goldfish pond, *Hedychium gardnerianum*, has a delicious scent, and exotic leaves, like most of the plants in this area. It is an area known quaintly as the dell, which does not sound exciting enough for a plant that comes from the Zingiberaceae family. Here, among a relatively new cornucopia of foliage, *Melianthus major*, with its plumes of greyish silver, contrasts beautifully with the flesh-like growth of *Beschorneria yuccoides*, a vulgar-looking thing: someone recently revealed to me that when in bud it *reminded* her of a donkey.

The other two main Fox gardens also have, near their houses, manifestations of the Victorian grotto scene: Trebah has its small but beautifully landscaped Koi carp pond, and at Penjerrick there are the remains of a conservatory described in the *Gardener's Chronicle*, sometime in the late nineteenth century, as

> a cave like passage which leads into what may be termed an underground grotto, with a skylight. It is here the filmy ferns are seen enjoying their situations as if they were in a state of nature, whilst the dripping fountains and pools of golden carp add to the beauty of this unique promenade.

This caused a French visitor to write, 'Anna Maria found her pleasure in the animal as well as in the vegetable world, monkeys, marmosets, cockatoos, paraquets and love-birds, avadavats and canaries, they were the inmates of her colony'. It must all have been quite busy.

Any treatise on the Victorian garden scene would be incomplete without a short digression on the subject of terraces. In the first place, for many Victorians the idea of lying in the sun was considered dangerous for one's health; in Falmouth verandas were the thing. In the second place, especially within the confines of a largely Puritanical family such a pastime, for any prolonged length of time, was bordering on the slothful. The likelihood was that neither the space nor the word 'terrace' on its own was often used. The photographic evidence is that there was simply raked

Penjerrick

gravel forming a path in front of the house, and a place where one could occasionally sit among a plethora of scented plants. Mariana Tuckett in her diary of 1858 says of Trebah, 'A broad terrace walk goes along the front of this new part of the house'. Again at Penjerrick there was a terrace walk which 'extends the long low rambling building, half-cottage, half-house', and beyond into its version of what George at Glendurgan had called 'the straight walk'. Barclay Fox records that the 'ladies… dined and tea'd on the walk in front of the house.' Here there were potted oleanders, and at Glendurgan wall shrubs such as abutilons, cassias, passion flowers, plumbago and the potato flower.

In 1904 it is recorded that at Trebah the front of the house was covered with flowering climbers, 'which include *Tacsonia mollissima… Tacsonia Volxemii, Bougainvillea speciosa… Cassia corymbosa* – which has nearly veiled the whole of a gable end, and the ivy leaved *Pelargonium* 'Madam Crousse'.' One progressed through and under these plants into the garden beyond, without the modern implication of this being an outside room. As seen today, the terraces at the three main Fox gardens are not original. At Trebah the front of the house is given a bold treatment of informally arranged granite blocks, osteospermum and agapanthus; at Penjerrick the low wall covered with cotoneaster and the terrace of crazy paving tie in perfectly with the period of the house, 1935. At Glendurgan in the 1960s the addition of a low, slate-topped stone wall was considered visually a great improvement, especially looking up from the valley as it arrests the appearance of the house slipping away down the lawn.

Penjerrick, 1868

From sitting inside the house, however, it steals a percentage of the view. What must always be borne in mind is the original design of the house and garden. Subsequent alterations to either have become part of their history, and reflect the needs and fashions of passing time.

Scentless, but for its exoticism not to be omitted, especially in a Victorian garden such as Glendurgan or Carwinion, where there is a national collection, is the bamboo. I suppose it is conceivable that one day I might enter a bamboo phase with more enthusiasm than, at present, I will visit a bamboo collection.

Yet I would be the first to complain if they were eradicated from the garden, especially the kitchen garden where they are invaluable as canes; and they can be planted with tremendous effect, for example edging the board walks along the inclines of the valley garden at Heligan. In the centre of Glendurgan, and in one

Heligan

Bamboo bridge

of the biggest clumps of bamboos, the stream used to be traversed by two planks covered with chicken wire. This has always been known as the bamboo bridge. But in 1995, as a mark of the National Trust's Centenary, the creation of a bridge made out of bamboo became a very successful project. This was very much the gardeners' own initiative, and it is to their credit that except for one or two large poles, the bridge was made out of Glendurgan's own bamboos, and put together using the best of local maritime rope-work.

There are two more unusual genera which deserve a mention for the way in which they contribute towards the character of the garden: *Quercus suber*, the evergreen cork tree from the Mediterranean, and *Eriobotryia japonica*, the Himalayan loquat tree which outside Cornwall is normally a shrub.

I am also fond of some plants that appear to be growing in the wrong place, perhaps left over from a former era, or perhaps scattered by a bird. No one knows why a martagon lily suddenly chose to appear in the long grass of Manderson's Hill. For years there was an inexplicable clump of *Aconitum* in the

Caroline Fox etched by Herkomer after a drawing by Samuel Laurence

cherry orchard – a wonderful blue in late summer. But in George's diary there is a helpful reference on 4 July 1920 to picking 'arums, purple and grey irises, monks-hood [*Aconitum*] and brick coloured lilies'. Also near the pond there used to be for years a small strip of *Narcissus poeticus* var. *recurvus*, which deserves to be planted in sheets rather than strips, as does a daffodil hybridized by George Johnstone of

Trewithen, and aptly named in all its elegant simplicity 'Caroline Fox', after Robert Were Fox's daughter of that name.

Narcissus Caroline Fox

Other treasures from the past have also disappeared: *Primula* 'Wanda' and *Convallaria majalis* var. *rosea*, the pink lily-of-the-valley so tenderly remembered by Graham Stuart Thomas as being my grandmother's favourite flower, emblematic of her and her love of flowers. *Rosa* 'Veilchenblau', plucked from a punt in about 1920, came from a riverside garden in Cambridge, but I shall never be able to trace the name and origin of an old rose that once climbed romantically up a rhododendron tree just to the west of the house; the nearest is 'Champneys' Pink Cluster', a name which sounds strangely inappropriate for both the plant and the place. Perhaps one day some of these lost genera may be restored, for they in particular carry the personal touch of different members of the family.

Tree ferns from the antipodes are fun. The ends of their fronds in spring resemble violins; there is an entire string orchestra in the lower regions of the garden at Penjerrick. The tenacious

Tree ferns
(*Dicksonia antarctica*)
at Penjerrick

Rhododendron ponticum lives on *Dicksonia antarctica* not parasitically, but epiphytically – in other words, on the water shoots which make up its trunk. Will the changes in climate result in tree ferns one day becoming as familiar as hydrangeas? For with their large, bright green leaves, and abundance of colourful flower heads, anybody on first acquaintance would have thought hydrangeas the most amazingly opulent plant.

Of the same prehistoric appearance as tree ferns is the maidenhair tree, *Ginkgo biloba*. It is of a remote family, and well known for its strange, fan-like leaves, but less well known for the fact that it is a deciduous conifer. Medicinally, it is taken to improve the memory. It has also has been discovered to contain a substance which is effective in the control of AIDS. In this respect the Eden Project near St Austell is remarkable for drawing our attention to the proprietorial values of plants – a subject which is beyond the scope of this book, but one which I have come to experience in different forms at Glendurgan, and one which was of tremendous interest to previous generations. Another very obvious example is *Agave*, valued in this country for its sculptural effect, but in South America, grown as a crop, it provides the raw material for the manufacture of sisal.

In New Zealand arum lilies grow wild. So does cineraria, in the startling colours of rugby football socks. Whereas campion, that most British of British wild flowers, is tended in their borders. Taking that perspective as given, it becomes easier to look at some of this country's wild flowers more objectively. Sometimes I have got out of the car to stare in wonder at a bank of wild flowers; and sometimes on the cliffs I have lifted my foot to count beneath it nine different wild flowers. As Barclay Fox wrote of Penjerrick, 'Spring is calling them forth in myriads, spangling the old borders & long walk-hedge with a prodigality of beauty'. But they do not have to be a crowd: the sight of one *Anemone nemorosa* is eternal. In the garden I never fail to be excited by the sight of a Ragged Robin, and once among the primulas I came across a single wild *Iris sibirica*, surpassing Solomon in all its deep purple glory. Not even the blackest acquilegia can compete with that.

CHANGE
THE FIFTH GENERATION
CHAPTER NINE

'They think we are too old – not that they say this in so many words – to make a new home and to have building cares and roadsmaking etc. I see their point of view & I know it is probably the right one – just because at first it hurt so – to give up the last tie – to that precious spot – but now it is all gone – and I have no wishes left about it – I think the cares are beyond us, & during the short time left us, we must not add to the weight of burdens our children will have to face hereafter. 'Already I feel I couldn't bear the fruits of selfish desires granted if they were not in the "right ordering". Sometimes one has to put the gift away without looking at it, but I have looked at it – & loved it and can part from the idea more easily – because of having held it for a moment or two as a bare possibility'

(Lucy Hodgkin to her brother George Fox, 27 July 1911)

View west up the River Helford from Rosemullion Head

These lines were written in response to an earlier invitation by George to purchase Glendurgan. Both Cuthbert and Moyra, and their son Philip, had come to recognize the reality of her words concerning the weight of burdens. But what she said was prophetic in other ways too. In 1989, 17 years after my grandfather, Cuthbert, had died, and a year after my grandmother had died, the sentiments of my parents must have been akin to Lucy's. The occupancy of the house had once again become a family issue, and although there was ample precedent for it to continue being a retirement home, my parents saw the sense in it being released to the next generation. So began a long process of renegotiation with the National Trust, not just for the house's continued occupation by a member of the family, but also for its transformation from a very dated building into a house more suited to the needs of a family living in the twenty-first century.

I was one of those children who, aged seven or eight, were sent hundreds of miles away to be educated at a private school. From the dormitory windows there was a view that, with an ounce of imagination, reminded me of Glendurgan. Sometimes, until the ringing of a school bell interrupted my dreams, I thought that it too would lead down to the sea. The magnitude of geography is sometimes hard for a child to grasp, and there were some poignant connections: nearby was a pub named 'The Falmouth Arms', after the famous Cornish family which had once owned the school as a private estate. At home I loved to walk out to Rosemullion Head, land purchased and given to the National Trust in memory of a school friend who in 1960 had died in a fire. His short life is commemorated by a seat, with spectacular views up the River Helford.

Why had I been removed from so much beauty and placed in an alien land, a land of red brick houses with bare boards and bright lights and iron beds? Would, could I ever return to the place I loved more than anywhere else in the world?

Often as I stood on the playing fields the only thing that played for me was the sound of the trains on the main line to Cornwall. It had a two-fold effect: the wheels going swish, swish, swish would ferry me quickly, but the mournful note of the train horn seemed to say 'Can't stop… can't stop'. Somehow it was different from homesickness; I was moderately happy at the school. This, in comparison, was just a change that I found incomprehensible. When I look back, it seems wholly suitable that the school's nightly prayer, 'Lighten our darkness', responded so well to its motto *clarior ex obscuro*.

But then at last the darkness lifted, and the holidays let in the light: humaneness, and dogs with friendly faces, and flowers, and old fashioned things, the smell of baking, soft Cornish voices, and the comforting sound of the sea, all waters as the shore.

Such are some of my recollections from school life, and such is the magnetic call that many Cornishmen feel for their roots.

Memories are often stronger than the actual event, and the passage of time can embroider the truth. Nonetheless there is no doubt that in the days of private ownership there was a much greater feeling of mystery, of adventure, and of pleasing decay, especially in the those areas which were not subject to regular maintenance. As a child such places were irresistible: beyond the rubbish dumps, the bottle tip and incinerator, places where the work of rats, rather than gardeners, was clearly evident, into the thickest woods where fallen trees were left to follow their own ecological course, into the foulest-smelling paint shed, down streams which flowed through tunnels of bamboo and laurel, on to the weed which caked the ponds, and into innumerable thickets of probably one of the biggest pests to the Forestry Commission: *Rhododendron ponticum*. (It is reported, however, that the purple acres of this plant at Lanhydrock did not pose a problem for its particular owners. On being asked what they did during the rhododendron's flowering period of May and June, when all Cornwall is ablaze with colour and looking wonderful, they replied that they simply escaped to London. Yet it was from school that we as children longed to escape, which was not as simple; and returning there at the beginning of the summer term we watched with sadness for our last glimpses of *Rhododendron ponticum* bordering the bridges at Bodmin Road.)

Rhododendron ponticum

Take any one area of plant invasiveness or pleasing decay and submit it to the treatment of modern professional garden management, and there is a dramatic change in a garden's overall character, as well as in terms of a child's appreciation. A few years ago my wife and I visited another Cornish garden, not open to the public, and several degrees worse than the descriptions above: towering trees of ivy, awesome rhododendrons the size and shape of tornados, conifers like skyscrapers, and hydrangeas and tree ferns like weeds. We were subdued into silence by what we saw, and by the vanity of our own gardening interests. As we trudged along several miles of wet, roughly ploughed field, actually a path, Caroline suddenly gave evidence of her half-Irish origins by saying, 'You know this is really much more my sort of thing.' But as

Tim Smit who restored Heligan has so successfully proved, pleasing decay does not last for ever. In that now unlost garden there is a potting shed where, by the smell of tobacco mixed with earth, onion and tarred string, one can be transported back to the days of one's youth. At Glendurgan there is also a potting shed, in fact a great array of purpose-built sheds and bays, as befits an efficiently run garden, but the best apple shed is now a holiday home, and the cattle-rush, which operated like a level crossing over one of the garden's main routes, and down which cows rushed to drink from the stream, is now what is known as a feature. In Durgan the telephone cables have been buried, and the National Trust's cottages have had their woodwork painted a discreet grey, a colour contrasting starkly with some Cornish estate cottages which are still in private ownership, and whose windows are picked out in mixed primary colours.

In order for the great English gardens to survive, there undoubtedly has to be some kind of income. Occasionally this may come from an internal source, but in many cases the only way to provide an income is to 'open to the public', words which to an increasing number of landowners must have all the resonance of a death knell. The consequence of this is the advent of several little buildings, which nowadays rejoice under the name of 'facilities'. The Duke of Bedford is reported as saying that in his opinion the success of opening to the public is largely dependant on 'teas, toilets and car parks'. Often these then become the

cause as much as the effect of increased visitor numbers; and in some cases, much to the annoyance but also the convenience of the purists, excellent facilities have become the focus of a visit. It is a trap of which the National Trust seems to be aware.

Nonetheless the pressures of creating 'dwell-time' are very real: obliging members of the public are unwittingly directed into areas where they might be persuaded to part with their money. Another tactic is to step up the level of interest for children in the shop, thereby assisting sales with 'pester power'. For some of us, thankfully, and to its own great benefit and uniqueness, a few places survive such as Penjerrick. It lies at the end of several little lanes, which are uninvit-

The cattle-rush

ing to the modern coach, and unlike many other gardens open to the public there is nowhere suitable, short of wrecking the park, for modern facilities. At present, cars are parked on the grass either side of the drive; admittance is through a creaky wrought iron gate, and admission is paid into a hole in the top of something labelled optimistically in black paint 'honesty box'. Such a modest approach is in dramatic contrast to the luxuriance of the garden. The *Gardener's Chronicle* in 1874 wrote of Penjerrick that it was 'the consequence of the unpretentious humility everywhere manifest which conquers one's inmost heart', and the same can be said of that garden today.

Penjerrick

Penjerrick

Penjerrick

The facilities at Glendurgan have been carefully landscaped to remain separate both in style and in location from the garden, the entrance to which is marked by two granite gateposts set in walls, each of which is surmounted by a statue of a running fox. The original foxes came from Wodehouse Place, the family house in Falmouth. Howard Spring, a local writer and friend of the family described them in one of his books as 'putty-coloured zoological improbabilities'. The public entrance into the garden is an attempt to emulate the original approach to the property, but there are a couple of differences to be noted. One is that the banks on either side have been filled with plants, and the other is that these plants are there for impact, a distant reflection in their way of what used to grow in the mixed and herbaceous borders of the walled garden. On balance it is a jus-

Wodehouse Place

tifiable compromise, but the uninformed should be told that the original entrance is bordered simply by the occasional shrub set in mown grass, perhaps uninteresting to a visiting member of the public, but historically much more in keeping.

I have not lived long enough to recall the days of citrus fruit being grown under glass, along with grapes and nectarines. I can, however, recall with clarity the vestigial days of the apple and pear trees, of medlars and quinces, and the productive days of the fruit cages in which were grown currants of several colours, dessert and cooking gooseberries, and raspberries. White peaches, protected by nets, were grown against the walls. Their consumption, the children were told, was for only the grown-ups, whereas the grown-ups were told that they were for only the children. Perhaps it is no wonder that we often came across wasp-infested peaches rotting on the ground; the children won in the end.

Our ears became accustomed to the sound of mowing machines and chain-saws; our eyes to the sight of grafting, layer and root; our tongues to golden tomatoes and varieties of fruit; our noses to the scent of blossom, and until the demise of the hives, our skins to the onslaught of bee stings. Once an entire swarm fell out of an elder tree on to the gardener's boy, with whom we had been playing. He survived the attack, but from then on we saw rather less of him.

Along the Schoolroom Walk there is a gravestone commemorating all the dogs that have ever lived at Glendurgan – 'a lot of names for one dog', a visiting child once commented.

Nowadays my father would take a walk in the garden with his Labrador and with, if ever there was a sign of the times, an instrument designed for the remote removal of canine defecatory matter. His father Cuthbert, however, was seldom without a large basket of cooking apples to be bestowed upon tenants or employees. Often accompanied by a grandson, and a dog, he would be on an errand to some distant apple store, or to an apple tree which bore a particularly good eater. I can hear him now, as he no doubt heard his father George, proclaiming, 'A pear is at its best for about twenty minutes during which time it may be seen to glow with a peculiar radiance by all who care to look.'

On some occasions we would be conscripted by our grandfather to assist with tying up the figs in little muslin bags. He was very conscious of the damage effected by marauding insects and birds to both fruit and flowers, and once in all sincerity asked a favourite cousin if she was ever bothered by blue tits in the winter. He was referring, should anyone be mistaken, to camellia buds, and not to the famous rhododendron which abides by that name, due to its resemblance in colour rather than its susceptibilities to the birds.

Another rather more serious mistake in identity he made, was during the Second World War when he was in the Home Guard, and had been posted to one of the little pill boxes that line the cliffs of the River Helford. One day he spotted a German in a tin helmet swimming up the river. In what must have looked like a scene from *Dad's Army*, he made contact with the local HQ, which presumably made contact with Whitehall. As a result, a full-scale launch was initiated, down the American-built army road to Trebah beach, and out into the river to surround the poor German at gunpoint – only to find the helmet was the shiny head of a seal.

I have a picture in my mind of my grandmother preoccupied with the picking and preservation of fruit. As children we used to pick our own, but nowadays we are invited on roadside billboards to 'pick your own', and therein is another change. I recall too her high standards: she insisted that one walked on planks in the herbaceous borders lest the soil was disturbed. She was an accomplished arranger of flowers. On one occasion a Polish visitor came to tea. The friends who brought him suggested that he should admire a particularly stunning arrangement in the drawing-room. With his face aghast, all he could say, in a heavily Polish accent, was 'I want the lavatory', which left my bemused and amused grandmother wondering if this was a genuine need or a Polish euphemism.

There used to be in the kitchen garden a few serried ranks of cutting flowers, such as larkspur and clarkia, grown specifically to be picked for the house. Camellias, often given to the local hospitals, could only be cut under her strictest supervision, surgically one might say; and once she said to me, 'You will be careful about this after I have gone, won't you?' To give another example of her high standards, years after she had 'gone' I came across the copy of a letter she had written to Michael Trinick, the region's agent, during the early days of the National Trust's ownership. The first side of her letter discourses pleasantly on spring colour in the garden, but on the second page the nub of it is reached. At that time the garden was open for a few days each week for a few weeks in the spring, and visitors were expected to park in the road outside the front gate, and to make a voluntary contribution because, in those immortal words, 'the cost of maintaining the garden is considerable'. One day my grandmother returned home, or was trying to return home, to find that access through the front gate, modest by any standard, was blocked by more than the usual three or four cars. 'Naturally' she complained, 'one sounded one's horn until the way was cleared'.

In the light of what has been said in a previous chapter about the garden's horticultural progress, some of the following changes can be viewed with a degree of irony, although it should be stressed that they are in no way a poor reflection on the expertise and dedication of the current gardening team.

No longer is the potting shed plastered with rosettes for prize-winning specimens, and no longer do gardeners return to work in the evening. In the Mawnan Cottage Garden Show of July 1918 Glendurgan's talented head gardener George Sanderson 'showed 20 exhibits, got 17 prizes all firsts in fruit except for green gooseberries – against five or six showing fruit'. No longer are there rows of vegetables to be harvested, 'washed and bunched', as my grandmother rather ruefully commented to my father a short time after the National Trust had become the new owner. Nor is there produce to be given away, or to become the object of the economical but mirky early morning walks of the hard-up trespasser. No longer are there Buff Orpingtons to be fed, or to be heard distantly beyond the trees. No longer are there duck eggs to be fetched from a hutch on the island in the pond, or asparagus to be culled from a bed measuring 65 feet by 15 feet in the walled garden. Nor does the garden any longer sing in winter with the joys of some of those sweet-smelling shrubs, *Hamamelis* x *intermedia* 'Pallida', *Chimonanthus praecox*, *Abeliophyllum distichum*, *Lonicera standishii*, and *Lonicera fragrantissima*.

On several counts a diary entry such as the following from 1915 would today be unlikely: 'finished picking ripe gooseberries… have had a splendid crop for three months R. E. T. sent staff to pick some two or three times to send to the Navy (sent free by the railway co.) of the Grand Fleet and had some for bottling for herself', and raspberries in those days were bottled with the ones on the outside of the jar facing outwards with a redcurrant inserted in each. No longer is a garden seat simply ordered from a catalogue, and no longer is a new drive 'laid out before breakfast', as was once recorded by Barclay Fox at Penjerrick.

No longer, in respect to and of Health and Safety are there paths beset by roots or rocks, mud or grass. But neither is the path behind the north wall of the walled garden maintained with gravel; nor does the adjoining border edged with box continue for the sole cultivation of shade-loving plants, in particular hellebores. The public's enjoyment and safety is understandably paramount. But in a hundred years from now will the old records of life at Glendurgan appear as colourfully descriptive as, for example, that of Mrs Belbin's accident? On 30 September 1918 she was

The road down to Durgan

bringing her bread van from Trebah to Durgan by the quarry road
leading horse by the wrong side, the wheel of other side went up
the bank and capsized upon her but edge of wheel caught on bank
and prevented it completely falling on her. Horse set off and only
stopped at the gate (reins getting about his heels). She called for help
and Durgan men Hendy and W. Pascoe etc released her from a very
perilous position. H. Pascoe says he has more than once warned her
for the sake of her horse and trap against coming down that very
narrow and very rough road when there is a good one available.

Will a world of increasing liabilities, packaged control and mobile telephones allow for the endearing response of Mrs Hext who, on hearing of a tree-felling accident in Glendurgan woods, brought from Trebah 'brandy and soup and

sent her chauffeur for a doctor'? Evidently those were the days before employees were trained in first aid. Nowadays during the summer the palm trees in the maze seem to be bearing an odd kind of fruit, actually buckets of some kind of delicious syrup, nectar to wasps and bees who otherwise become a source of distress to those who walk between the laurel hedges. To keep the maze panic-free these are no longer four to six feet high, and the earth paths recorded in 1912 have gone; and the handles to the ropes on the Giant Stride have all been lowered to a child-friendly height. No longer is there a lawn tennis ground in the Well field, which has become absorbed into a public car-park. No longer are there red squirrels whose natural habitat is Scots pine, as was so extensively planted by Alfred, and later by his son, who in 1925 had asked in his diary that 'they keep pineaster on show for many a year to feed the squirrels'. The family kept a pet squirrel, which was in the habit of entering the dining-room, climbing on to the table, and helping itself to whatever was available. So audacious did the forays become that one day a fork which was aimed at the intruder missed its target and removed a piece of wood from the table: an exercise in marquetry now marks the spot. As for the squirrel, curiosity got the better of him, or her: death by accidental drowning in a water closet is recorded. The disappearance of the red squirrel cannot, either, be levelled at the shelter belts of today, a well-researched ecological mix of woodland ecotone in place of solely pine, and in fields where ponies and donkeys once grazed. Talking of which, it is a quirk of fate that in the absence of the donkeys that helped to maintain the front lawn in weedless bright green grassy stripes, this area has now become a haven for wild flowers cropped short into the appearance of a lawn. Were this to be a complaint, one only has to look at the precedent of that most noble of gardens, Chatsworth, where large acres of lawn have similarly been dedicated.

No longer is the blackthorn edging the road down to Durgan adorned with hand-washed laundry set out to dry (see photograph page 104). No longer are there rotting dogfish on the rocks at Durgan, where the medieval stench of drains and ash pits have had their day, where metal baths no longer hang on the doors of outside privies, where several permanent tenants have now been replaced by holiday lets (my grandmother feigned unfamiliarity with this word 'holiday'), and where boats and wind-surfing boards are sometimes for hire, and the beach is no longer monopolized by family friends or relations. These are not criticisms, for there are constructive reasons for all these changes; they are merely comments on the era in which a National Trust garden now lives. What has been noticeable is the sheer excellence with which the Trust, and in particular the gardening staff, have responded both to the change and to the preservation of anything historic or idiosyncratic. For example, the cobbling and draining of paths in respect to Health and Safety, but in a manner which is unique to Glendurgan, are commendable. One of the most rewarding things to see in the garden is the way in which the gardeners are motivated by a project, but perhaps this is occasionally a case of the tail wagging the dog: no one wishes to sweep up leaves for ever.

Furthermore, it has to be said that omitted from this list of changes are countless solutions to a sea of problems with which the family had to contend on a fairly regular basis. Many of these, thanks to the National Trust, have now disappeared. Drains, or rather the lack of them, always used to be rather 'iffy' if not sniffy; one particular lady said to my father, 'I would rather stay as I am than pay extra rent for sanitary facilities.' Staying as she was, as most of the villagers had been doing since the year dot, but are not now, meant outside loos and ash pits, requiring regular inspections by the landlord or his agent, and for those without an ash pit, a strong ebb-tide. These arrangements resulted in a log of complaints tedious beyond belief for someone like George who had better things to do. Amid so many entries referring to the state of privies it is refreshing to come across one that refers to ducks 'messing about the village to the annoyance of others'. George writes about the responsible but irresponsible tenant, 'She was indignant about it,' no doubt like the ducks, 'but I was firm'.

For a period there were lengthy negotiations with the family's cousins, the Tucketts, over boundaries and over the conveyancing of land in between their property, Bosloe, and Glendurgan. Now that the National Trust owns both properties it has not been slow in establishing and increasing windbreaks on that side of the garden. Neither has it been slow in improving the magnificent open view to the mouth of the River Helford from Bosloe, which has become one of its premier letting properties.

Bosloe

A typical example of the Trust's ability to think laterally, and their gardening staff to act with resolution, is that the granite posts which were fixed in 1914 to mark the boundary between Debell Tuckett's land and that of Glendurgan have now been transported to form a distinctive fence edging the field next to the main car-park.

Parking has always been a bone of contention, and must have caused untold stress to George's peace-loving nature. Many users, but non-residents of the village, assumed proprietorial rights. Presumably it was with this thought that the record of condition dated 1912 says, 'The road to Durgan and boundaries either side are in a bad state of repair. I understand that this has been left so purposely to discourage traffic down it and that it is desirable that the road should remain in this condition'. Times, however, change and for years after its relevance in 1923, there was on the wall of one of the cottages a notice that read 'Motors or vehicles are not allowed to be left in this village unattended by their chauffeur or driver'. Times, however, changed again, and it is to the Trust's credit that it recognized the problem of parking, grasped the nettle, and converted a field into an informal type of car-park for visitors to Durgan and its neighbouring beach of Grebe. Again, as regards the condition of the road, indeed the condition of anything, the Trust is very ably equipped to deal with issues of pollution, the environment, and wear and tear, let alone the complexities of local planning law, which at one time took up much of George's time. Dealing with trespassers also trespassed on his time; paradoxically this seems to have decreased now that the place has become more accessible.

In terms of ownership and management, Glendurgan is a National Trust garden. But in terms of concept, inspiration and sentiment, it is still very much a Fox garden. The family did not have the benefit of horticultural expertise, yet it created a perfectly harmonious garden, which evolved by trial and error, as well as by the application of aesthetic considerations. Neither did it have the unlimited sums of money, and the single-minded motivation which in the last few years has arisen among many private garden owners, and which must be causing the National Trust to sharpen its horticultural pencils. If the Trust places any value on its own admission that its properties achieve their unique and particular characteristics through the realization of a single family's creativity, then the Trust, in the truest sense of the word, should, and does, welcome the family's involvement. This is especially true in the instance of any of the garden's ingredients being in vehement contradiction to the family's taste: it leads to a confused image for visitors, generally something not to be experienced at Glendurgan. In any event, if ever this does happen the donor family has to respect the decisions and the responsibilities of the National Trust. In an ever-changing garden the only constant factor that will maintain its special character and its individuality rather than its conformity, is the continuity of purpose behind the aesthetic influence. This, like the garden, may change and progress from generation to generation, but it will remain constant in its application and its appreciation of the garden.

However, some questions have to be asked. To what extent should the progress of a garden be impeded by either a family's amateurism, or its bad taste? In the instance of another famous National Trust garden, Tintinhull, to what extent should progress be accelerated by the occupation of a tenant who happened to be a professional gardener endowed with exquisite taste? To what extent should any trust wrap up a property so that change can never be instigated? If this had been the case, perhaps 300 years ago, would this country have such a glorious inheritance? If something has been entrusted, then surely change should be resisted? But then does not the spirit of innovation, which created these places, suffer from repression? How and when fossilization should be applied is almost a form of art in itself. It is ironic that often the same authorities that seek to preserve monuments from the past are the ones who seek to arrest their introduction today. The tragedy is that occasionally a new monument, in the name of making history, does get past all the planning and preservation bodies, and then arrogantly stands in all the new clothes of a twenty-first-century emperor for anyone and everyone wonderingly, and wondrously, to applaud. The same is also woefully true with works of art, to the mystery of some but the complete fallibility of others. What controls, what ombudsmen, are there available on the one hand to prevent stagnation, but on the other to prevent properties from becoming coated with the veneer of one organization's taste and methods, any more than the veneer of one council's response to popular demand or fashion? For example, in the instance of the National Trust, and admittedly to its great benefit, a large number of roses must have crept into their gardens as a result of one of their garden advisers being an expert on the genus. Or, never mind garden advisers, to what extent should any National Trust garden be keeping up with garden fashions as proclaimed by the media (railway-sleepers are popular), and imbibed with ever-increasing thirst by the masses?

As everyone knows, the propensity for a fashion to date is immense, and this is as true in the gardening world as in any other world. A few years ago the latest vogue was *Corydalis flexuosa*; then it became *Cerinthe major* 'Purpurascens', and as for roses one can almost predict what the next popular verdict is likely to be. In the 1960s it was 'Kiftsgate', but this is now overtaken in the race of climbers and ramblers by scores of French ladies. *Tweedia caerulea*, with its truly sky-blue flowers, once caused eyebrows to rise at Chelsea Flower Show, but is now available at the local garden centre, along with a vast range of plants which 40 years ago had to come from specialist nurseries. Sometimes there is a deserved degree of pity for some of these beautiful plants as they pass in and out of fashion. In particular, one which has become lampooned as the florist's flower, on every restaurant table and every grave, is the *Dianthus* which, if viewed objectively for a moment, is a stunning plant. Perhaps that is why it has become so popular and so well known – the Mona Lisa of flowers. Beautiful beyond words to me on any count, carnations cannot fail, especially the old fashioned malmaisons, the size and shape, and often the varying degrees of colour, of cricket balls; and in anyone's garden there can never be too much of the ageless *Alchemilla mollis*, or *Euphorbia characias* subsp *wulfenii*.

Should features in gardens necessarily always be the result of features in magazines? Where is the dividing line between a worthy introduction and gimmickry? At Glendurgan a middle-line has been drawn, where both conservation and innovation work in harmony; where the past has been interpreted discreetly. An exposition of this is the Valley Head path, which was an inspiration of the family, approved and implemented by the National Trust, and now looking as if it has been in existence since the garden was first created. More recently, following the dramatic restoration of the maze to its original design, there was a problem with members of the public who either wished to leave in a hurry, or could not find their way out of it. Consideration was given to the introduction of signs. This idea was discarded eventually in favour of my idea of planting four palm trees, each one to be placed in an existing horseshoe of laurel, roughly located in each corner of the maze – from an article in the *Bath Weekly Chronicle and Herald* in the 1930s it is evident that on the original plan there were further rustic thatched houses in these positions. There they stand, the Alhambra effect, acting as signposts for those whose ingenuity has been tried, more than for those who wished to try their ingenuity. In the face of this break with convention and tradition, the National Trust and its advisers have resisted any temptation to replace the hut in the middle with what had adorned the original maze in Bath: a revolving wheel swing, an eighteenth-century version of the London Eye, offering useful views over the unhappy wanderers. To be really faithful to the original, the National Trust could in addition construct an underground passage from the centre of the maze to a nearby moss-covered grotto – the quick exit. It is to the Trust's enormous credit that, on the whole, it can remain judicious on issues of innovation and conservation.

The timber eyrie high up on the east side of the valley, with a deservedly good view of the maze, is not original, although in the record of condition dated 1912 a rustic chair at the top of five wood steps is described in the plantation to the south and east of Manderson's Hill. On a grander scale, but with the same purpose, there is on the east bank of Trebah's main valley a worthy

View from
timber eyrie

Alice's seat, Trebah

Alice's seat, Trebah

restoration of a triple-breasted summerhouse, which
may have its origins in Charles's day, but which has
come to be known, strangely, as Alice's seat, after Mrs
Hext.

But for some the making of history is preferable to the preserving of it. The upturned boat at the top end of the Cherry Orchard is a modern interpretation of what originally served Alfred as a shelter and store when he first started tilling the ground as a vegetable patch. But Alfred was a modern man: the maze which had inspired him from the Sydney Gardens in Bath was barely 20 years old, and he would be the first person to recognize that vegetables and fruit are no longer grown in the Cherry Orchard. The only edible thing left is an old mulberry tree, outshone now by magnolias and a neighbouring *Metasequioa glyptostroboides*, which came to this country in 1947. Waterproof clothing allows gardeners to garden in the rain; tools have to be kept under lock and key, and if unable to commission plants from abroad Alfred would certainly have trotted off to the local garden centre.

There is a handsome re-creation of the old schoolroom on the far side of the valley in Birch's orchard, a plausible idea in that it reminds the public of the original character of the place, and also of the family; but again, except for the original Georgian neo-Gothic windows, it is all brand new. Earmarked for educational purposes – an increasing role the garden has to play – it is not in fact fulfilling its original purpose any more than beautifully restored orangeries were intended to be tea-rooms. Although the nature of the original edifice has been painstakingly researched and reproduced by the National Trust, the modern building is inevitably a much better construction in comparison with its tumbled-down predecessor, which would have stepped out of any Victorian picture of a woodland cottage, being approached by teacher with child in hand, through drifts of rose-bay willow-herb rather than the existing *Ceanothus* and choice conifers. What is impressive is the way in which the current head gardener, Steven Porter, and his team, have dauntlessly set about improving the views from and to this new edifice. Unknown to the public, but delightfully in keeping with the traditions of the garden, has been the involvement of the local schoolchildren in the construction and opening of this building. The Trust's readiness to do this, incidentally, and also to invite children on other occasions, such as its Centenary, or the opening of the maze, reflect a change back to the very early days when the presence of children played such a vital part in the history and character of the garden. More recently a new area, in the vicinity of the schoolroom, has been landscaped specifically for groups of children and their educational needs.

The schoolroom.

The schoolroom at the head of Birch's Orchard

For some the 'unmaking' of history has its attractions. This poses a serious problem for those listed houses that find that a hideous modern staircase is as eternally listed in mothballs as a medieval window. Fortunately gardens cannot be exhibited in time capsules – something which was probably not fully realized at the time of the gift of Glendurgan to the National Trust. The ephemeral nature of gardens does allow for change, and for the making of garden and gardening history. That, if nothing else, validates this book, which aims among other things to describe the garden at the time of its being donated to the National Trust compared to what it has now become.

Nevertheless, there are a few examples of plants I would like to exempt from any historic listing; or have they become part of the garden's history? The golden conifers, *Chamaecyparis lawsoniana* 'Lanei', halfway down the valley on the east side, have been observed by their brilliance to steal the eye. But it could be argued that they represent the 1970s, when my grandparents in their old and golden-wedding-anniversary-age suddenly developed a

Chamaecyparis lawsoniana 'Lanei'

modish attachment to gold and green; they even bought a golden-green car, in addition to planting an impressive hedge of *Hypericum* 'Hidcote'. Years earlier my grandmother, on her arrival at Glendurgan, set about increasing the heather at the bottom of the main lawn, in order to remind her of Scotland. Why? It is reminiscent of other places too, and although native to the area and of the same family as rhododendrons, *Ericaceae*, it is really more suitable for a heathland-type garden, such as the National Trust's Castle Drogo in Devon, rather than a woodland valley garden. What has saved this area has been the Trust's ready response to the suggestion that it should feature some unusual heathers, and enough of them to create some impact.

This is how gardens are made, and in the years to come the bright ideas of today will go in and out of popularity. A horrific example of this is the Japanese knotweed, which was introduced to Britain as an ornamental plant, but which has now revealed

Erica carnea

its true character as being totally invasive and able to grow through concrete and dislodge gravestones. No wonder it seems to like building sites. A bright idea from Glendurgan is the so-called rockery – a pile of old mineral and metal specimens that once formed a grotto, 'a prominent and objectionable object', Sarah Fox commented disparagingly at the time of its construction (so for critics of the National Trust, even in the days of private ownership there was not always a conscensus).

There are those who might regard some of Glendurgan's at present embryonic gardening plots and plans as genetic engineering; others will see them as progress; and in the passage of time these views might alternate. In the end who are we in our littleness to tell, despite all the growing number of experts and advisory bodies? For when all is said, which I deem it now is in this book, what is it that moves me to take an interest in gardens, let alone to try to write

about one with which I have had close associations? It is not the plant enthu-
siast who bends double with his magnifying glass in the examination of some
rare fern. It is not the writer, photographer, artist or garden designer intent
upon the capture of some idea. It is not a romantic notion either of gardens
being the ultimate goal in the perfection of our life on this planet, or of its flowers being like actors in a play. It is simply a God-given instinct, inherited from
my forebears and aptly described by Wordsworth:

Thanks to the human heart by which we live,
Thanks to its tenderness, its joys, and fears,
To me the meanest flower that blows can give
Thoughts that do often lie too deep for tears.

('Intimations of Immortality',
from *Recollections of Early Childhood*)

APPENDIX 1
PLAN OF GLENDURGAN

KEY
1   Camellia Walk
2   Cherry orchard
3   Maze and pond
4   Manderson's Hill
5   Lower valley
6   Durgan village
7   Birch's Orchard
8   Giant Stride
9   Schoolroom Walk
10   Holy Corner, or Heavenly Bank
11   Valley Head path
12   Schoolroom
13   Viewing platform
14   Cattle rush
15   Dog grave
16   Alfred's boat

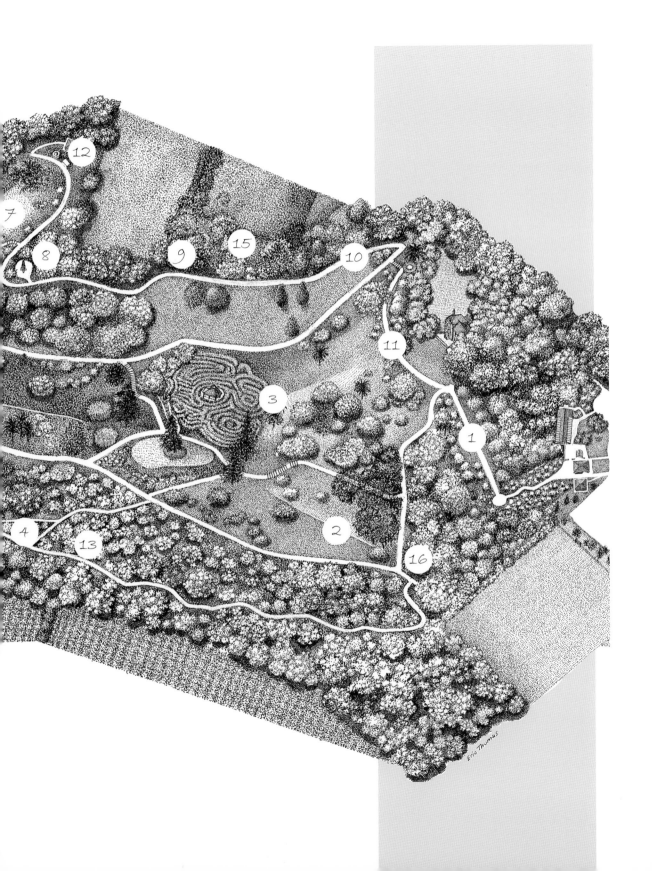

APPENDIX 2
SIMPLIFIED FAMILY TREE

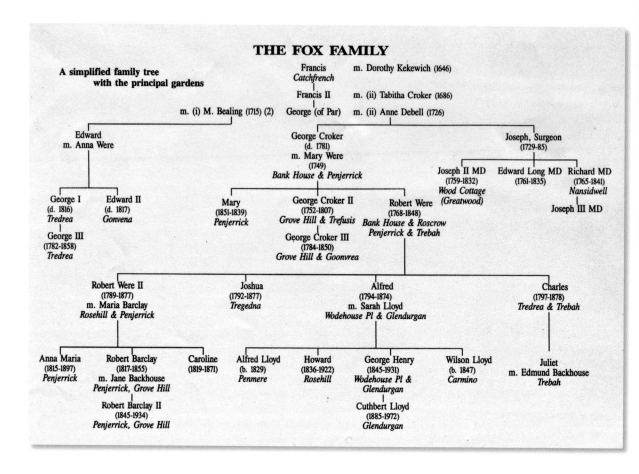

APPENDIX 3
FAMILY CONNECTIONS

BOSANQUET

Ellen Sophia, 1875–1965. Daughter of Lucy Anna Fox and Thomas Hodgkin, married Robert Carr Bosanquet, and author of a book of memoirs – Late Harvest.

FOX

Alfred, brother to Robert and Charles, married to Sarah Lloyd.

Their children were:

George, 1845–1931. Lived in Falmouth at Wodehouse Place, and also at Glendurgan. Married to Rachel Juliet Fowler, 1858–1939.

> **Their children were**
> Barnard, 1883–1894
> Cuthbert Lloyd, 1885–1972
> Dor, Dorothy Juliet, 1887–1937
> Ann, Annette Sarah, 1889–1981
> Erica Mary, 1893–1934
> Meg, Margaret Veronica, 1895–1976
> Romney, George Romney, 1898–1968

RET, Rachel Elizabeth, 1833–1923. Married first a cousin, Samuel Lindoe Fox, and second Philip Debell Tuckett, whose descendants came to own Bosloe, a neighbouring property to Glendurgan, on the road to Durgan.

Howard, 1836–1922. Lived in Falmouth at Rosehill, which was later given by his two daughters, Olivia and Stella, to Falmouth Borough Council to become eventually part of Falmouth College of Art and the public gardens known as Fox-Rosehill.

Lucy Anna, 1841–1934. Lived at Treworgan, Mawnan Smith. Married into the Hodgkin family, who rank both eminent artists and scientists among their members.

Theodore, 1831–1899.

Wilson, 1847–1936. Lived in Falmouth at Carmino and married twice into the Rogers family who owned Carwinion, Mawnan Smith.

Mary, 1835–1892. Married to Sir Joseph Whitwell Pease Bart.

FOX

Charles, brother to Alfred and Robert, married to Sarah Hustler.

FOX

Elton, Samuel Middleton, 1856–1941, author of *Two Homes*, and son to Samuel Lindoe and Rachel Elizabeth Fox.

FOX

Elton, Joshua, brother to Alfred, Robert and Charles, lived at Tregedna where, according to his niece Mariana, he grew 100,000 roses. He married outside the Quaker sect.

FOX

Robert Were, brother to Alfred and Charles, married to Maria Barclay.

Their children were
> Anna Maria, 1815–1897
> Robert Barclay, 1817–1855
> Caroline, 1819–1871

FOX

Philip, son to Cuthbert and father to Robert, Charles (author of this book) and William.

PEASE

Sir Joseph Whitwell Pease Bart, son-in-law to Alfred and Sarah, married to their daughter Mary (1835–1892).

TUCKETT

Mariana, 1807–1863, daughter of Alfred's sister Mariana , married to Francis Tuckett. Her diaries were edited by Hubert Fox, and published privately as *Mariana's Diary: A record of a holiday at Falmouth*.

A note on measurement
Imperial measurements are used throughout this book.
1 inch = 25.4 mm
1 foot = 12 in = 0.3048 m
1 yard = 3 ft = 0.9144 m
1 mile = 1.609 km
1 acre = 4,840 sq. yd. = 0.405 hectare
Money
Pounds, shillings and pence are used throughout.
£1 = 20 shillings (20/-)
1 shilling = 12 pennies (12d)

First published in 2004 by
Alison Hodge
Bosulval, Newmill, Penzance, Cornwall TR20 8XA
info@alison-hodge.co.uk www.alison-hodge.co.uk
Reprinted, with revisions, in 2005

ISBN 0 906720 35 4

British Library Cataloguing-in-Publication Data
A catalogue record for this book is available from the British Library.

Designed by Christopher Laughton
Originated by BDP – Book Development & Production, Penzance, Cornwall
Printed in Singapore

The publishers have made every effort to trace copyright material,
and regret that in some cases this has not been possible.